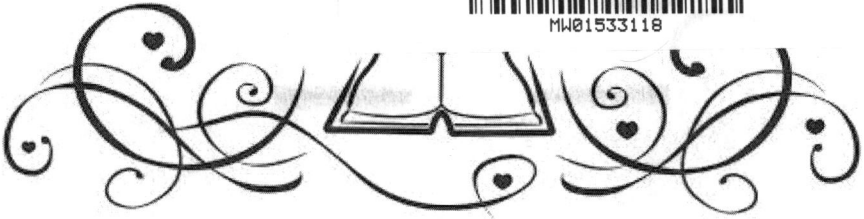

# IT'S A
# MIRACLE

## God's Amazing Miracles

Phillip & Joanna-Coe Herndon

# All rights reserved

All Scripture quotations, unless otherwise indicated, are taken from the *King James Version* of the Bible.

ISBN: 9798752006975
Imprint: LeonHeart publishing Inc.

# FORWARD by Bill JOHNSON

The Israelites were exhorted to train their children and grandchildren on both God's Law and on the report of His wonderful works. They were to continually share the testimonies of God's miraculous power with the next generations.

Psalm 78:5 says that the Lord, *"established a testimony in Jacob, and appointed a law in Israel, which He commanded our fathers, **that they should make them known to their children;** that the generation to come might know them, the children who would be born, that they may arise and declare them to their children."*

There was a value system for the spoken and written record of all that God had done, which was to be passed down from generation to generation.

The following verse tells us why: ***"that they may set their hope in God,** and not forget the works of God, but keep His commandments."*

There is something intrinsic to the testimony that teaches us to place our hope in God in the face of trails. When we've been raised hearing about God's supernatural interventions, trusting Him is a natural reaction to life's challenges. We may not understand what He's going to do or how He'll do it, but we've seen Him move. We've heard the stories. We know His heart for us. We can be confident because the soil of our hearts has been seeded with the truth that God is faithful in impossible situations. The testimony of God's love and power sets the stage for us to have the courage to walk in radical obedience to Him.

Too often, miracle stories slip back into our spiritual history. The other common danger is that we begin to think of them as only happening to other, more famous people. They usually lived some time ago, or on some missionary field. That kind of thinking is a dangerous, downward spiral. When we share testimonies less frequently, we begin to see fewer miracles. The fewer miracles we see, the less we come to expect them, and the less we share the testimonies. Miracles are not mere memories; God's wonder-working power is our current reality. And testimony invites us into a relational journey where we learn to take His promises and risk everything to see Him do it again.

I'm so grateful that Joanna Coe has invested the time and energy into collecting the testimonies from both her father's ministry and her own ministry with her husband, Randy (Phillip). The chapters in *It's a Miracle* are not just exciting testimonies that happened to a well-known revivalist long ago. These sometimes shocking, yet beautiful stories carry the revelatory heart and nature of God. They invite us all into a greater understanding of our personal relationship with Jesus because they are records of God's loving covenant with us. Once we've seen the weighty and powerful love of God, we know that only a miracle could fully represent it.

Our testimonies are not personal rewards. They are records of a God who is willing and able to work through all of us, an imperfect people. He looks for people who have a value for his nature and who will give him an opportunity to do what He does best. We get to be a part of that incredible journey. As you read this book, grab ahold of every sickness healed, every creative miracle and every instance of restoration. This is God's heart for you and for those around you. Let these stories stir up your faith. We were designed to invade the impossible, just like our Father. **Bill Johnson - Bethel Church, Redding, CA**

**Author of: *Open Heavens* and *Born for Significance***

# ENDORSEMENTS

## Dr. Michael H Yeager, Jesus is Lord Ministries International Inc

*This book is a MUST read, filled with wonderful, amazing Miracles, healings, and signs and wonders. I have known the authors of this book for over a decade and have watched as God has used them to bring Miracle after Miracle into the lives of those they have prayed for. Faith will come alive in you as you read this amazing book. As you are reading these encounters with God, it is like reading a continuation of the book of Acts. I highly recommend this book, as it will radically change your life forever.*

## Dr. Ron Charles, Missionary to Egypt

*The best way to determine a person's dedication to God is to view their life at home, away from the pulpit. I have known Randy and Joanna Herndon for several years. I can truthfully say that their lives are consistently Godly, whether at home or at church. As such, God has used them in miraculous ways to bring healing to the needy and deliverance and hope to the oppressed. This book is a true record of how God has used them for His purposes.*

# ACKNOWLEDGEMENTS

We would like to thank many who have encouraged us and helped us write God's miracle stories. We hesitated because we felt there were so many books in print and didn't think another book was needed. But we realized that all testimonies and God stories are so important that we needed to stop procrastinating and share with you, the readers, to build faith, encourage, and let you know God still heals and does miraculous miracles today. Your stories, and the miracles that God has done for you, are so important to share with others. We hope this encourages you to tell your stories.

We want to personally thank Dr. Michael Yeager for helping us get this together and helping us with writing, printing, and putting together this book.

Holly Bickel for taking time to read and make corrections.

Thank you to Bill Johnson, Dr. Ron Charles, and Dr. Michael Yeager for their time in reviewing and writing forwards and endorsements.

There are not enough words to thank all of you for helping us, loving us, and encouraging us.

We pray this book is a blessing to many, but more than anything, we pray for you to receive your miracles, healing, salvation, and deliverance.

# IT'S A MIRACLE

# TEACHINGS

These are teachings and experiences are from the lives of Randy and Joanna (Coe) Herndon. This book is written for those who truly hunger and thirst after nothing but the TRUTH that **God** has made available through the life, ministry, sufferings, death, and resurrection of **Jesus Christ**. Our prayers are that not only will your life be touched by these **Miracles divine Truths**, and **Experiences** but you yourself will truly step into the truth that sets men free. **God** is not a respecter of people, what he has done for **one HE desires to do for others**. May you experience wonderful freedom, Transformation, divine healings, and **Miracle**s from the hand of **God as you read this book**.

## PS: All the stories are being told by Joanna, unless otherwise noted!

# EXHORTATION

When things start exploding and getting exciting, God does not want you to miss what He is doing. You don't want to hear somebody tell you about it after the event, you want to be right in the middle of it. At least I do. I want it to be my story, not their story.

This book is full of stories that my husband and I have experienced. These are God's supernatural divine healings and interventions. You will also read some of the stories of my father, Jack Coe Sr., who was mightily used of God in the healing movement in the 1940's and 1950's.
What God did for my father, and what He is doing for my husband and I, is available for you too. You see, God is not a respecter of people.

*"Then Peter opened his mouth, and said, 'Of a truth I perceive that God is no respecter of persons.'" Acts 10:34*

*"For there is no respect of persons with God."*
*Romans 2:11*

Not only is God not a respecter of people, but what He has done in the past, He will do it again, and again, and again. The Scriptures declare that God does not change, and neither does Jesus Christ.

*"For I am the Lord, I change not; therefore, ye sons of Jacob are not consumed." Malachi 3:6*

*"Jesus Christ the same yesterday, and today, and forever." Hebrews 13:8*

We are sharing our testimonies because we overcome Satan by the blood of the Lamb and by the word of our testimony. We also know that this will cause faith to arise in the hearts of the readers. We believe that there is a **Miracle** waiting for you in the reading of this book.

It is important, however, that we do not seek the **Miracle**s, signs, and wonders, but seek the **Miracle**, sign, and wonder giver. His name is Jesus. The more intimate we get with Him and the more we get into His presence and learn how to flow with Holy Spirit, the more **Miracle**s we will see.

*"And they overcame him by the blood of the Lamb, and by the word of their testimony; and they loved not their lives unto the death." Revelation 12:11*

# IT'S A MIRACLE

# CONTENTS

# CHAPTER ONE
# IT'S A MIRACLE

It was a shivering, cold, winter night in the month of February in West Lafayette, Indiana. Snow was covering the ground. I was the speaker for the *Season of Grace* conference. I was nervous and shivering inside myself because I wanted to preach what God wanted spoken.

We returned to our hotel room that night, after preaching on *The Cry God Responds To.* Now, instead of praising God for helping me get through it, I began to cry out to God to tell me what to speak the next night.

The next day I was studying and crying and saying, "God, tell me what You want me to speak tonight!" At that very moment my phone rang. It was my friend calling and she wanted to show me her new house and tell me more about all the great things that God was doing in her life. I thought, 'I do not have a sermon for tonight, and I do not have time to visit,' but being a good friend, and because I enjoy being around her, I went to her house.

God had blessed her beyond measure. She now had a two-story house, which was three times bigger than her previous house. She would squeal, **"It's a Miracle!"** as she took us from room to room. She showed us things she had bought, and things people had given to her for her new place. Each time in a voice of excitement and joy she would jump up and down and say over and over, **"It's a Miracle!"**

I kept thinking, 'I do not have time to be doing this. I need to get back to my hotel room to prepare a message for tonight.' But it was so exciting to see all the great things God had done for her and how she was so blessed. Her excitement was contagious.

When I finally got back to my room to study, those words kept ringing in my ears. **"It's a Miracle."** I could not shake this declaration from my mind. Now when we think of the word **Miracle**, we think of healing, signs, wonders, and the miraculous. We think of the stories like when Jesus turned the water into wine, or when He fed the five thousand, or walked on water or raised Lazarus from the dead. We think of **Miracle**s like when the blind eyes were opened, or when the lame walked and the deaf heard. But I began to realize there are

**Miracle**s all around us every day in our life.

The snow, the grass, the birds, the flowers, herbs, sky and so much more. These are the natural glories of God. In First Corinthians, it tells us about these God-given natural glories. It is God manifesting His love to all of humanity.

*"There is one glory of the sun, and another glory of the moon, and another glory of the stars: for one star differeth from another star in glory."*
*1 Corinthians 15:41*

Then there is the supernatural glory, the **Miracle**s of God's divine interventions. When He saved my soul, which is the greatest **Miracle** anyone will ever experience; that was a **Miracle!** When He healed my body more times than I can remember; that was a **Miracle!** When my marriage was on the rocks and Jesus restored our relationship better than it ever was; that was a **Miracle!**

When the Lord put money into our mailbox when we desperately needed it; that was a **Miracle!** When He supernaturally put money into our bank account; that was a **Miracle!** When He gave us a financial raise at work; that was a **Miracle!** And when He gave us a bonus financially at work; that was a **Miracle!**

Now think about all the **Miracle**s that God has done for you. When God sent groceries to your house when your cupboards were bare; that is a **Miracle!**

3

You are breathing right now; that is a **Miracle**! This declaration, **"It's a Miracle,"** went deep into my heart. I realized that this was my message: **"It's a Miracle!"**

This was when I looked up the definition of **Miracle**.

**1)** *An extraordinary or astonishing happening that is attributed to the presence and actions of an ultimate or divine power!*

This is speaking about Jesus Christ. This book you are about to read is full of amazing examples of God's divine healing and **Miracle**-working power.

**2)** *An event that appears inexplicable by the laws of nature and so is held to be supernatural in origin or an act of God.*

You better put on your seatbelts because this book is full of amazing, divine, inexplicable, and unexplainable **Miracle**s.

**3)** *Something which man is not capable of making happen and which is therefore thought to be done by God.*

This is the divine touch and the ability of Jesus Christ, the Father and the Holy Spirit performing these, **Miracle**s.

# FOURTH STAGE CANCER HEALED

My friend, Angela, from Pasadena, Texas told me a story about her friend who had fourth stage cancer. She said that it was a very aggressive cancer. The doctors told her she might have three more months to live, but really there was no hope for her. She was dying and it was evident because she had become so frail and so tiny. She told her husband that she wanted to go to church. He loaded her up in the wheelchair with all her medical hookups.

It was on this Sunday that the Holy Spirit moved mightily upon the pastor's wife. Uncharacteristically, the pastor's wife stood shaking and crying under the power of the Holy Spirit. Now, this is not something that she typically did.

The pastor's wife boldly declared, "Everyone sick and who needs healing come quickly! Jesus is here! Come NOW! Come to the altar!"

At hearing this declaration from the pastor's wife, the husband of the lady who was dying from fourth stage cancer grabbed her out of her wheelchair, with her hookups flying everywhere. He ran as fast as he could with her in his arms up to the altar.

Immediately this lady began to feel better after being laid upon the altar. Her hunger came back, and she started eating.

They took her back to the doctors. Three weeks later the doctors concluded, through lots of tests, that there was no cancer. They could not find any cancer cells in her body anywhere. The doctor informed them that people do not live through this kind of cancer. The doctors wrote on her file: **"It's a Miracle!"**

# MY FATHER JACK COE

My father was Jack Coe, and I am so excited to have his legacy in my life, but I'm excited also because he taught me about Jesus, and that Jesus does it all. He taught me about the Holy Spirit and fire. My earthly father knew the **Miracle**s and healing that was made available through Doctor Jesus, and through the Holy Spirit.

He used to always tell the people, "It's not me; it's Jesus, and you can do it too." So, it is not about my name, but it's about the name of Jesus Christ. My dad went from being an alcoholic to saying, "Hot dog, I got it!" God ended up giving him the largest tent in the world back in the 1950s (the tent held 22,000 people inside, with another 10,000 to 20,000 standing outside), where many divine **Miracle**s took place.

What you are reading in this book are not Randy and Joanna's **Miracle**s. They're God's miraculous **Miracle**s. We were just a vessel used of God and a witness to them. Every one of you reading this book, you are God's miraculous **Miracle**. Go ahead and say, **"I Am a Miracle!"**

# DYING BOY HEALED FROM ASTHMA

I met a lady close to Erie, Pennsylvania. She came to one of my meetings around 2014-2015. She told me that she had attended my dad's tent revivals in Erie. This was back in the 1950s, when he was holding a tent revival in that area.

She told me, "My son had real bad asthma and almost died several times. I heard of the **Miracle**s in your dad's tent meetings and said, 'I must take my son there.' When I got to the meeting, I discovered there was a massive group of people. Brother Coe told the people to form up in the line so he could pray for them."

She said, "As I stood in line waiting for my son to be prayed for, I saw a man right in front of us who your dad spoke to with great boldness. Your dad said, 'Stick out your tongue!'"

She then told me that my dad took his hanky out of his pocket, and pulled it across the man's tongue, and said, "You demon of cancer come out!"

She said, "Right there in front of our very eyes, that cancer fell off on to the white hanky. He showed us the cancer on the hanky. I was right there, and I saw it all. Not only that, but my son was healed of his asthma that day."

She kept on attending his meetings even after her son was healed. She told me that every week in these meetings there were so many coming out of wheelchairs, that they had to stack the wheelchairs outside the tent. She said they stacked as high as a mountain, and every week they had to take them out to burn them and destroy them. They were making room for more coming out of wheelchairs. **"It's a Miracle!"**

# STOMACH TUMOR DISAPPEARS

In one meeting as my father was ministering, he spoke to a very large woman. He told her, "Hold on to your dress!" His words were so full of authority and the power of God that she instantly grabbed a hold of the top of her dress and held onto it for dear life. My dad reared back his fist and hit her in the stomach very hard.

Now, my dad was no little man. He was six feet tall and over 300 pounds, so when my dad hit her hard it was no little punch. When he hit her that hard it should have killed her, but instead, God showed up. Everybody in the tent gasped for air as they watched my dad hit her. But right there in front of everyone's eyes this woman instantly lost five dress sizes. I mean instantly her body weight shrunk.

My mother told me later, "When your father did this, I thought, 'Jack, what in the world are you doing?'" But then my mother saw this incredible instant **Miracle**.

It turns out that the woman had a humongous tumor in her stomach and when he hit her hard with his fist, the tumor was instantly gone.

Later, they asked this lady how she felt when Jack hit her, "Did it hurt?"

She said, "No, not at all. I didn't feel anything."

**"It's a Miracle!"**

# CRIPPLED MAN RUNS

In one of my dad's tent meetings, he went to a man in a wheelchair. When he got to the man, my dad grabbed him and pulled him up out of the wheelchair. Then he kicked the wheelchair away from the man, so the man couldn't sit back down.

My dad said to this man, "Walk in Jesus' name!" When my dad let go of this man, he fell to the ground. My dad picked him up again and said, "Walk in Jesus Name!" This man hit the ground again. My dad picked this man up again and boldly said, "I said walk in Jesus' name!"

For the third time this man fell to the ground. The next time my dad picked him up and turned him around. Then he literally kicked this crippled man in his rear end, boldly saying, "**I SAID WALK IN JESUS NAME!**"

When my dad kicked this man, he stumbled forward, and it looked like he was going to fall to the ground, but instead he took off running. He ran all over that tent shouting and praising God.

You might ask, 'why would your dad be so rough with the crippled man?' You need to understand it was not my dad, it was the Holy Spirit that was upon him and moving through him mightily.

When the Holy Spirit comes upon you that way, you do not even think about what you are doing or saying, you simply act. Then, and only then, will God confirm that you are hearing from heaven. **"It's a Miracle!"**

# A WOMAN RAISED FROM THE DEAD

In another one of my dad's tent meetings, he had prayed for a woman on a hospital bed. Then he continued to go pray for others.

Someone came up behind my father and tapped him on the shoulder and said, "Brother Coe, the woman you prayed for has died."

My dad said, "Where is she?"

When they brought the lady to him, she was lying on the hospital bed with blood on the sheet. Because she had died, someone had pulled the sheet up over her body and the top of her face. He threw back the sheet with divine boldness.

Before anybody could protest, he picked her up over the top of his head and then he threw her into the air shouting, **"I SAID LIVE IN JESUS' NAME!"**

Her feet landed on the platform, and when she did, she began to spin like a top. At that very moment she came back to life. Everyone who was in this meeting saw this incredible **Miracle**. **"It's a Miracle!"**

# A BOLD MAN OF FAITH

My dad was a bold man of faith. He broke crutches, stepped on glasses, and pulled people out of wheelchairs. Sometimes he would hit them, slap them, and do things that would seem to be violent, but it was not him. It was the Holy Spirit in him.

You see, God hates sickness and disease. Jesus Christ paid the ultimate price for our healing and **Miracle**s. The sufferings of Jesus are not meant to be in vain. My dad loved people deeply. He was not trying to hurt them or be mean to them, but he was setting them free by the authority and the power that is in the name of Jesus. One day Oral Roberts was speaking to my dad. He said to my father, "Brother Coe why do you do these things to the people?"

My dad said, "I am not hitting them or slapping them, it is the devil that I am hitting and slapping. I break the crutches and jerk them out of the wheelchairs because I know God is healing them, and I do not want them to rely on those crutches and wheelchairs anymore. I want them to believe and have faith and rely on Doctor Jesus, the healer.

# JESUS STILL DOES MIRACLES

The recorded **Miracle**s that Jesus performed are only a fraction of the people who were touched and healed by Jesus Christ. They were acts of love and compassion. He healed them not to show off and to prove himself, but He healed these people because it was God in Him that was healing, delivering, and setting the people free. Jesus declared everything He did was to reveal the Father.

When Jesus shows up it is characteristic of Him to heal, deliver, save, and set the people free. He never comes to a meeting or to you and says, "Oh, so you need a **Miracle** healing? I'll be right back, I left that at home." No! It's characteristic for Jesus to heal right then. He declares, "**Arise and be healed!**"

**Miracle**s are not merely superhuman happenings, but happenings that demonstrate God's power, and who He is. Almost every **Miracle** Jesus did was a renewal of fallen creation, restoring sight, making the lame to walk, even restoring life to the dead.

Believe in Him because He is the son of God and because God is continuing His creation. He does not only heal His people but even those who are sinners. He heals the needy, the poor, the weak, the crippled, the orphaned, the blind, the lame, or some other desperate need.

**Miracle**s, by their very nature, defy scientific explanation. Defining a **Miracle** is like defining infinity or eternity. It is impossible for us to know all the mind of God, and therefore it's impossible to understand all His ways. **Miracle**s can never be understood by the natural mind, they can only be accepted, and believed.

When is the **Miracle** coming? The **Miracle** is here right now because Jesus Christ is here with us right now. God wants you to be a **Miracle**. He wants you to receive your **Miracle**. Jesus wants you to be healed, delivered, and set free by His miraculous healing power. Freely we have received, freely we need to give.

*"Heal the sick, cleanse the lepers, raise the dead, cast out devils: freely ye have received, freely give."*

*Matthew 10:8*

# GOD SHOWED UP THROUGH A DVD

We make DVDs available of my father's meetings. In one of our meetings a lady purchased a DVD of my dad's tent meeting. In that tent meeting there were many amazing healings and **Miracle**s. She decided her neighbors needed to come watch them with her because they had such a wonderful impact upon her. She went around her community inviting as many neighbors as she could to her house to watch this video.

These people were Baptist, Methodist, Episcopalian, Catholic, and other different religious denominations.

She told them, "Listen, do you want to see **Miracle**s? Do you want to see people come out of wheelchairs? Do you want to see blind eyes open? Then come on over to my house tonight, and I will fix you dinner, and afterwards we're going to watch this DVD."

Her neighbors agreed to come over. She made dinner and after they were done eating, she put on the DVD. When my dad said, 'Raise your hands and praise the Lord,' on the video, this lady said that all the people in the room raised their hands and praised God like my dad told them to. When my dad said, 'Stand up now and praise the Lord,' she said, "They all stood up in my living room, lifting their hands and praising the Lord."

This lady said, "We watched that and began to immediately see **Miracle**s. God showed up right there in that front room touching the lives of the Baptists, Presbyterians, Catholics, and others." In the video they watched as people came off those stretchers, and hospital beds, and out of wheelchairs.

She said, "Some of the people in the video who had cancer and lupus and different other diseases, we saw them get healed."

When my father went home to be with the Lord, plus other well-known men like him, such as AA Allen, William Branham, Oral Roberts, and more, **Miracle**s did not stop happening.

These men were not the **Miracle** workers, they were simply the vessels through which Jesus Christ manifested himself. Jesus wants to manifest himself through you too. What Jesus has done for us; He will do for you! **"It's a Miracle!"**

# TAKING AUTHORITY OVER A HURRICANE
**(Randy Herndon)**

How many of you believe that prayer can change the weather? I have prayed for that many, many, many times. There is one time when a hurricane was headed right for us while we were holding a church service. It was in New Jersey, and that hurricane's name was Irene. It was coming right to the Jersey shore.

As the service was going on, one guy was upset and worried as he was watching the TV. We all decided to continue to have the service knowing they were evacuating the area. We were all in there having a really good time in the Lord. This man wanted to evacuate, but his wife wanted to come to the service first. He brought her and told us we were all crazy for staying. He said the national guard was going around asking people to evacuate.

Joanna, my wife, said, "Well, we're just going to pray that God will turn the storm away from us." She said, "I need to know the direction Irene is coming to us."

She then had everyone stand facing the way the storm was to come into the area. She told everyone to point their hands out and we were going to pray for this to turn away from us.

So, we got everybody to pray, and then Joanna went back to preaching. All of a sudden, we heard this guy in the living room start yelling and screaming. He was jumping up and down. He ran into the room where we were conducting the meeting and he started yelling. He said, "It's turning, it's turning!"

Thank God it did turn away. Yes, even a hurricane had to turn away when you're standing in faith in the name of Jesus. **"It's a Miracle!"**

# YOU WILL NOT HURT MY CAR

We were in Louisville, Kentucky, and we had just finished preaching and praying when the lights started flickering.

Everyone began saying, "Quick! Quick! Everybody to the basement quick we are being hit with a hurricane!" So, everybody just runs down to the basement. Well, not me.

My husband said to me, "What are you doing?"

I said, "We got a brand-new car out there. I don't want no damage done to our car." So, I ran outside to where the vehicles were parked.

Randy was like, "What are you doing?" He was right behind me following me.

I got outside into the parking lot, and I began to declare, "In the Name of Jesus, you will not touch this car!" As I was saying this I was pointing at our vehicle. "You will not touch our vehicle, no scratches, no damage, no nothing."

Now, this straight-line 90-mile-an-hour wind was coming straight for us. It was the remains of hurricane Ike that had moved all the way up into Louisville, Kentucky while we were there. I mean, it had come all the way from Texas.

So, I'm out there just praying, and the church people are hollering at me. Even one of the ministers was yelling, "Get her in here!" Well, they did not stop me.

That hurricane was not going to destroy our new vehicle. I said to the storm, "Peace, be still. Jesus, You said we could speak to the storms. We could speak just as He did. God, you lead by example, in Jesus' name, peace be still."

While I was praying, telephone poles were flying in the air. The roof of the building next door came off and flew past me. The electricity was going off everywhere. They finally got me down into the basement.

We never lost electricity in that church. They don't understand how that can be. The people did not understand how we had electricity. And when we came out, nothing touched my car or the two to three cars to the left and to the right. Other people had wood and trees thrown inside their car. Some of their cars were twisted and mangled and ours was just sitting there as beautiful as ever.

The one guy (Pastor Johnnie Beard) who was hollering to grab me and pull me down into the basement, said to me, "Thank you that you stayed and prayed, because my car was next to yours and it did not receive any damage; just like yours."

We need to rise up and say, "No, you're not going to do that in the name of Jesus. You're not coming here." **"It's a Miracle!"**

# GET INTO CRASH POSITION

I love to travel by plane, train, and automobile. Sometimes I go to Canada 2 to 3 times a year. One of the churches I go to a lot there is Jehovah Jireh.

I am not afraid of flying, but I heard an Apostle friend of mine say one time that he always prayed before he got on the plane. He said he would inquire of Holy Spirit about the flight and safety. I thought that was a great idea so I would put my hand on the plane to pray every time before boarding.

It was a beautiful day with the sun shining bright. The weather was perfect. The meetings in Canada were so awesome. The presence of the Lord was there. The people's lives were touched with physical and inner healing. I was so excited about what all God had done and was so caught up in thinking about how great it all had been, that I forgot to lay hands on the plane as I boarded.

I remember looking out the window at the clear skies and looking up to the sky thanking God for such a great time in His presence. I said, "God, not only did we have great meetings, but you have given me such a great day to fly home."

Then it hit me. "I forgot to pray and ask You if everything was going to be okay on this flight."

Then I heard like a small voice say, "No, it's going to crash."

I thought, 'that was a dumb thought, it's beautiful outside and everything is great.'

I heard it again, "It's going to crash!" I tried to brush off that thought because it didn't fit with everything going on.

I said, "Lord, if you are warning me so I can pray then I do not want to ignore this small voice."

I begin to pray for the hand of God to protect us,

angels to encamp about the plane and the blood of Jesus to protect us. Then I heard the pilot come over the loudspeaker system and told us they were rerouting our flight to a closer airport. It was the Tri-Cities airport. I asked the stewardess where that airport was located. She told me, but I could see the fear in her eyes. I asked her if everything was okay.

She said, "No, we are losing oil pressure and losing it fast."

I told her I would pray and that we would be okay. Then, in less than five minutes, the pilot came on the loudspeaker and told us we were not going to Tri-Cities but changing to Alcoa airport in Tennessee. I thought, 'Oh good my cousin lives close by there and I can go see them.'

The stewardess began to walk from row to row telling everyone to get in crash position. I heard her tell the lady in front of me to put her child in her lap and how to hold her and lean forward. Then she stood at our seat and said to get in crash position and was explaining how to do that.

I said to her, "We are going to be okay. We are going to make it."

The stewardess said to me, "Ma'am, lean forward and get into a crash position." She was trying to show me how to lean forward and do it correctly. She said, "Take those glasses off your head and lean forward now."

I said, "Okay, but we're going to be fine."

She said, "Do what I say!"

I said, "Okay. Okay," and I did.

We got into the crash position. During this whole time, I was declaring the word of God. I was saying, "Peace be still and protect these people and do not let fear overwhelm them. I rebuke the spirit of fear."

I remember the story of apostle Paul in Acts 27 where he was on the ship and had warned the people not to set sail or the ship would crash. They didn't listen and went on with Apostle Paul in the boat. Paul began to pray and give instructions to the ship crew.

He told the crew, ***"And now I exhort you to be of good cheer; for there shall be no loss of any man's life among you, but of the ship. For there stood by me this night the angel of God, whose I am, and whom I serve, Saying, 'Fear not, Paul; thou must be brought before Caesar; and lo, God hath given thee all them that sail with thee.' Wherefore, sirs, be of good cheer; for I believe God, that is shall be even as it was told me."*** **(See Acts 27:22-25)**

In other words, Paul was saying, 'I am on this ship, and you will not die because before me stood an angel of God that said I will stand trial with Caesar and God will spare your lives because I requested prayer for you. God is not finished with me.'

I reminded the Lord of that story and said, "God, I do not feel you are finished with me yet." I had inquired of the Lord and knew I wasn't going to die. I begin to pray, and I said, "Lord I do not want to crash. Jesus, you can stop this plane from crashing. I do not want these people hurt or the child in front of me hurt. I don't want my purse and suitcase thrown all around and I don't want to have to try to find all my stuff and my lipstick. Bring us all in safely."

I begin to declare, "We are all going to be okay because I am on the plane, and God is not finished with me yet."

At that very moment a spirit of peace came into that plane. I cannot explain it to you. No one was fearful acting or talking out loud. There was such peace that you knew it was going to be okay.

The pilot came on the intercom and said, "I don't know what they have told you, but I think I'm going to be able to land at Alcoa airport safely."

When we landed, this one lady turned around who was in front of me and she said, "Thank you ma'am, when you started praying, I felt such a peace overtake me."

Somebody else hollered, "Who was that who was praying? That peace overtook me too."

Pretty soon other people on that plane were saying the same thing. I told all of them that it was Jesus

Christ. Jesus was on that plane with us.

They kept us on the tarmac in the plane for 2 hours trying to check the instruments on the plane. This was a small airport, and they weren't sure about how to handle customs for us. The pilot kept telling them we had already gone through customs in Canada. They wanted to see if the plane could be fixed on the runway and send us on our way, but they finally decided to unload us at the Alcoa airport.

The pilot explained all he could to us about how we were losing oil and losing it fast, but all of a sudden the oil gauge froze, and he wasn't sure if we were losing oil or not. But if the gauge wasn't frozen and the reading was correct, he may have enough oil to land us.

We were all excited to be alive. I asked to stay a few days in Tennessee to visit my cousin. They were happy to arrange that for me.

When I returned back to the airport a few days later to fly home, an airline worker recognized me and said, "Were you on the plane from Canada the other day?"

"Yes, I was," I replied. "Is the plane okay and just instrument mal function as they mentioned?"

She said, "Oh no, honey. That plane is in the hanger all torn apart. They cannot understand how y'all landed safely with no oil." **It's a Miracle!"**.

# IT'S A MIRACLE

# CHAPTER TWO
## WE HAVE AUTHORITY

We have power and authority. We need to take authority over anything that is contrary to the will of God in our lives. Remember the devil comes to steal, kill, and destroy; but Jesus came to give you live and life more abundantly.

---

**"The thief cometh not, but for to steal, and to kill, and to destroy: I am come that they may have life, and that they might have it more abundantly."**

**John 10:10**

---

Miraculous things can be happening constantly in your life because He who is in us is greater than he that is in the world.

The supernatural in the believer's life is supposed to become natural. When God sends you to places, things start happening because you showed up.

People get spared. Their lives get saved. It's because we're there obeying God. God, the great healer, provider, and protector overrules the natural world. To the believer, believing is a fact. All things are possible to them who believe.

Set your mind on things above, because I'm here to tell you that **Miracle**s, by their very nature, defy scientific explanation. One thing that is impossible, is to explain to people how a **Miracle** works. It is God who is the **Miracle** worker and God is doing a **Miracle**. We cannot fathom His ways. **Miracle**s can never be understood. They can only be accepted. You and I can only be the receiver of what God wants to do.

## EIGHTY-YEAR-OLD CRIPPLED HEALED

I remember the story of the lame man in Acts Chapter 3. He was at the gate beautiful and had been laying there for many years. Everybody knew this man was lame and he was begging, but one day Peter came, and he said, *"Silver and gold have I none, but such as I have, I give thee, and in the name of Jesus Christ of Nazareth, rise up and walk."* (See Acts 3:6.) Immediately this lame man leaped straight up and started walking, leaping, and praising God.

How exciting it is when God heals people supernaturally. I'll never forget a number of years

28

ago when we were ministering in Pittston, Pennsylvania. The church had advertised that it was going to be a healing meeting. There was an older lady who came to the meeting, and they had to help her out of the car. She had a walker to help her get around.

Now at this church, they have these steep stairs that go straight up from the front door of the church into the sanctuary. They don't even have a resting spot from the bottom to the top of this long flight of stairs.

I was thinking, 'She's come for the healing meeting, how are they going to help this woman get up the stairs?'

Well, it turned out that they had one of those little electric chair lifts you can sit in, and it would take you up the stairs. This contraption was located at the back of the building.

When they saw the problem, they took her around the building in her little walker and they brought her up the other staircase. They finally were able to get her into the sanctuary of the church. Now, she wanted to be on the very front row. The people that were with her helped her as she wobbled her way down to the front of the church.

In most churches there are people who will almost fight for the back row. There are very few people who will fight for the front row, but that is a whole different message. This lady wanted to be on the front row. When I was finished preaching, I walked right over to her, and I said, "Are you ready for a **Miracle**?"

She said, "That's what I came for tonight."

I said, "Do you believe that God's going to heal you?"

She said, "I do."

I said, "Well, then I believe with you."

And we began to pray for her. When I was done praying, I said, "You are set free."

I did not know what was wrong with her. I did not even ask her what was wrong because there was about fifty to sixty more people waiting to get prayed for. She was just the first one I approached for some reason.

I told her, "It's time to get up and run." I said, "the man in the book of Acts Chapter 3, when God healed him, he stood up. Then he took off running and leaping and jumping and praising God."

Nothing happened at that moment. She just sat there and said, "Okay."

Well, I walked away from her, and I went on praying for people. Suddenly I began hearing this screaming and this hollering that was taking place. Someone ran over to me and said, "Look! Look! You're missing it!"

They held an iPad up in front of me, and on the screen, was this lady on the front flight of stairs of the church.

Here is what happened if I understand correctly. This woman said in her heart, 'Okay, this woman preacher told me to get up and start running. She said that is what happened in the book of Acts with the lame man, leaping and running. In the name of Jesus, I am going to do this!'

Not exactly sure how this all happened but when I turned around and looked, where she was sitting, she was gone.

It turned out that she went over to the steep stairs in front of the church, and she began running down the stairs, and running up the stairs, running down the stairs, and running up the stairs.

Now what was amazing was that this lady was 80-something years old. Now that had to be the Holy Spirit, because even though I'm healthy, I can't do that. Every time I have to climb a large flight of stairs I say, "God, just give me a little bit of that energy that the 80-year-old woman had that got healed in Pennsylvania."

I was told later that this woman continues to have a lot of energy and strength. I never found out what all was wrong with her, but she came in mangled, twisted and hurting, and she left completely healed.

# AT A PROPHETIC CONFERENCE

We were in a place in Branson, Missouri, at a meeting where there were some well-known prophets. At that time Randy and I were new to the ministry of these people. Even though we just barely knew them, and they barely knew us, they had decided they wanted to book us into this meeting. If we understood correctly, it was a prophetic conference.

We were not quite sure about going but they insisted that we must come and minister there. We prayed and we agreed to go to this meeting. At the end of one of the meetings, they had these different ministers and prophets come up front. They also had us come up front.

When they had these prophets separated, they told those who were attending the meeting to stand in front of the person you want to pray over you in a straight line. So, here stood all the prophets in a row. These people were coming to get a word from them. They were to the left and the right of us.

Then they positioned Randy and me. They told us to take the middle section. This building we were in was a large theater. It had steps that came down to the front, and on this flight of stairs there where different levels.

As we took our position in the very middle, the Lord told my husband, "Everyone in your line is going to be healed."

Randy said to me, "Honey, guess what!"

I said, "what?"

He said, "The Lord told me everybody who comes to us in our prayer line is going to be healed!"

Of course, we were the unfamiliar people at this prophetic conference. All the prophets were well-known ministers to the people there.

There were about fifteen or so people that ended up in our prayer line. These other well-known ministers had anywhere from fifty or more people in their prayer lines. Those who had put on the conference informed the people that if you need healing, get in the line with Randy and Joanna Herndon. They did not say if you need a prophetic word, because at that time we were not known to operate in prophetic words, even though sometimes we do.

Of course, these prophetic ministries also operate in divine healing, but the people were going to them for a specific word from the Lord. Remember this was a prophetic conference, and most of these people came for a prophetic word. Healing most likely was one of the last things on their minds.

Randy said to those in our healing line, "God told me everyone we pray for tonight will be healed.

In this same meeting there was a healing that really stood out to us. God did something that really amazed me. There was a woman there who was in her 80s. When she came to me as people were getting lined up to be prayed for, she said, "Honey I cannot stand."

I told her, "That is okay, go sit over there in a seat." I pointed with my finger where I was indicating. I told her that when we were ready for her, we would come to her, and pray for her. She took her little walker and wobbled her way over to the seats, and she sat down.

We first prayed for a girl's back and God healed her. During that time of praying for these people we prayed for shoulders and necks and knees. Praise God, all these people were getting healed in our line. It was exactly what God said He would do. He said, "I'm going to heal everyone in your line."

In fact, the healings and the **Miracle**s were so evident, that the next night, most of the people were getting into our line to be healed.

It's kind of like in the ministry of Jesus when the report went out that people were being healed, even more people came.

So, when we got to this lady with the little walker, my husband began to pray for her. Suddenly she said, "I'm on fire! I'm on fire! You are burning up my legs and my back! It feels like everything is on fire!"

Randy told her that it was the Holy Spirit that was at work in her. The power of God was doing a mighty work within her body. Instantly she was made whole.

She must have kept that fire through the whole conference. Every time I saw her after that she was running up and down those stairs in that theater.

The next night I saw her, and I said to her, "How are you feeling?"

She said, "Watch this," and she took off running up and down those stairs inside the place.

When this **Miracle** happened, I was much younger. I said, "Well, let me try that." It only took two times up and down those stairs to tucker me out. Here was this lady in her 80s under the power of the Holy Spirit, and the fire of the Lord, running up and down these stairs like she was an athlete.

Sometimes God not only heals you, but He energizes you. He gives you supernatural strength. That is a supernatural strength with a supernatural healing. That's why sometimes when people get healed, they leap and run and jump and get excited. **"It's a Miracle!"**

## SLAMMING HER KNEE AGAINST A CONCRETE WALL

Seeing people healed is so exciting to us as ministers. Just looking at their faces when they are sick and tormented, and then suddenly God shows up. You see it in their faces, body motions, and responses. The response is so precious that when we see God touch them, it sometimes brings tears to our eyes.

We were in Duncan, Oklahoma, and we were praying for people. There were people getting healed everywhere, backs and necks, and people falling out under the power of God.

Some of them would get excited and they would take off running around the church. They would be showing everybody in the church what they could do. They would be saying, "Look! I got healed! I got healed!"

Now, this one lady kept watching and watching. Then she finally came up for us to pray for her. You could tell as she walked that she was in tremendous pain. She told us that she had just had surgery on her one knee, but something was wrong.

She said, "I need my kneecap and knee healed."

I said, "All right, well come sit down on the altar." I said, "just sit down here," pointing to the location."

There is just something special about the altar. It is where people kneel, shed their tears, repent, get saved and commit their lives to Christ.

She sat down on the altar. She then raised up her pant leg and showed me her fresh surgery stitches.

I said, "You just had this surgery done?"

"Oh Yeah," she said, "just a few days ago."

She said, "I don't know, is it too late to get healed because I had this surgery done instead of looking to God?"

I told her, "It's never too late for God to heal."

My husband and I laid our hands on her leg. Suddenly she cried out, "My leg is on fire! It is so hot!" Then her voice almost turned to that of being accusative. "What have you done to me?"

I told her, "We did not do anything to you." I said, "Usually when the fire comes, that represents the healing power of God."

When God begins to work in this way, I say what my dad used to say, **"Hot dog I got it!"**

Many times, through the years when we have prayed for people, we hear the report of them experiencing the heat and fire. That is the time to begin to shout, '**Hot Dog You Got It!'**

So, I asked this lady, "How do you feel?"

She said, "It feels good!"

She stood upon her feet and began to check it out. I thought, praise the Lord, and I walked away from her and went on to pray for some other people. As I was praying for these other people, I glanced back to where she had been, and here she was running back and forth.

After a little bit, somebody came over to me indicating there was an emergency. I basically asked, "What is wrong?" They informed me that that lady I prayed for had lost her mind.

I said, "What!?"

They said, "She has gone wild!"

I looked over at her, and here she was at the wall of the building which is made of concrete. She is literally taking her knee that I prayed for, and banging it against the concrete wall, over and over.

I went over to her, and I asked her, "What are you doing?"

She said, "Well, I just want to make sure that it is healed!"

She said, "Before you prayed for me it really hurt. But now I have no pain, even with banging it against the wall."

I am like, "Well you could hurt it by doing what you are doing."

She assured me she was okay. I thought, 'well she

is an adult, so I will just leave her alone.'

I went back to pray for the people, and I was thinking as I walked away from her, 'I don't know what the doctor's going to say when you tell them that you were banging your knee against the concrete wall.'

Can you imagine the doctor asking her questions? "You went and got healed at a church meeting? They did what with your knee? You banged your kneecap that has just been operated on and still has stitches in it against a concrete wall?!"

Well, it is hard to believe but none of the stitches came out, and the kneecap was not damaged.

That woman, when she was done testing her knee, came back over to me and she said, "I'm Baptist."

I said, "You are?"

She said, "Yeah, but I think I like you Pentecostal people." She said, "You know what? Just to let you know, I do like you Pentecostal's. I am going to act like you." She started jumping up and down, and then she started running around like some of the people in the church.

She came back and said, "I could never do this before. I couldn't run. I was always in terrible pain."

I said, "Well, don't go banging your knee on the wall no more, Okay? Just run all you want."

I went back the next year, and I asked the pastor, "Where is the lady who had the surgery on her kneecap? You know the one who kept banging her knee against a concrete wall?"

I mean, that really troubled me, that a person fresh out of surgery was taking their knee and banging it on the concrete wall. I was like, 'DON'T DO THAT!'

I wanted to go tell her stop it, but she was so excited. Even when I tried to talk to her about it, she said, "It's okay. It doesn't hurt."

I told her, "Okay, but I really wouldn't do that. That's not very wise." See, we need to use common sense.

I said to the pastor, "What about that lady that banged her knee on the wall? Do y'all hear from her?"

"Oh yes, she goes to church here," the pastor told me. "Do you see all these paintings hanging on the church wall? She is the one who painted them for us. She also helps teach the children and helps teach the teenagers."

God got ahold of that woman that night, and she has never been the same. Not only did her knee get healed, but her heart got healed, her mind was healed, and she was completely transformed by Jesus Christ. She also received the Holy Spirit. **"It's a Miracle!"**

# YOU HAVE GOD'S ATTENTION

We were in Pittston, Pennsylvania and there was a young girl there in the meeting. I went up to minister to her, and she had a cast on her foot. I went over to her, and I said, "You're not going to like what I'm going to tell you, but I am going to tell you that God wants to heal that foot, and He wants to heal it tonight."

The Holy Spirit gave me a word of knowledge for this girl. I said to her, "You really do not want it to be healed because you get a lot of attention from this because of the condition of your foot." In fact, I was looking at the cast on her foot. I told her, "I see everybody at school has autographed your cast. It is like you wanted them to, and they did. So, you really don't want it to be healed at all!

You want to keep this attention because you have a lack of getting the right kind of attention. You do not get the love that you are longing for. You do not get the attention you've been wanting. But God told me to tell you that He's been trying to give you the attention that you need. God wants to give you the right kind of attention. He wants to show you that you will get more attention from a **Miracle** healing than you will from suffering from your foot injury."

See, there's some people who want to hold on to their sickness and stuff because they need that attention. Other times they do not want to be healed because they need the money coming in from their disability. I have had people tell me in the healing line that they did not want to be healed, they just simply wanted the pain to stop. They tell me, "I don't want to get healed because they'll cut my money off."

So, I continued to tell this young lady, "I'm going to tell you right now, you'll get so much attention, you won't know what happened. Even the doctors will be surprised how quickly it has healed."

She said, "Really?"

I said, "Yes, you will get more attention than you could ever imagine. Now, would you like to get healed? Are you ready now to pray and get healed?"

She said to me, "Just pray."

I prayed for her just like she asked me to. Now, at that moment, it did not seem like God had heard my prayers, but the next day we found out that the Lord did touch her. The next morning, we showed up at church early because we had to conduct three services that day.

When we pulled up, there was this young girl standing at the front door. She was jumping up and down with excitement. We found out that she had taken the cast off the night before after we prayed for her.

She said, "Come here and watch this." The stairs up

to the church were steep and long. She ran up the stairs, on that foot that had been broken, like it was nothing. Not only was she running on that foot, but she was jumping on it.

Then she told us, "It is exactly like you said. Everybody is paying attention to me because of this **Miracle**."

She's got a testimony that gave her attention. She was sharing her testimony wherever she went. It was a miraculous testimony of God's healing power that heals broken bones.

At the same time, God wants to heal broken lives. He wants to heal the disease, plus our problems, and to take away the torment. God wants you not only healed of the disease and the pain, but even what is wrong on the inside of your heart and your soul.

After we left, sometime later I received good reports about this young girl. The pastor told us how she was going out and witnessing to many people about her healing and Jesus Christ. It all happened just because she finally realized the right kind of attention, which is God's attention.

You do not need man's attention. They cannot do anything for you but give you a pity party and that doesn't change anything. God will not show up at your pity parties. You might as well stop it.

In Luke 15, we read about the story of the prodigal

son. When the brother of the prodigal son was having a pity party outside, the father had to go out to him. The older brother felt sorry for himself because he had never had a party.

The father told him, *"Son, you are always with me, and all that I have is yours. It was right that we should make merry and be glad, for your brother was dead and is alive again, and was lost and is found." (See Luke 15:31-32.)*

When people get right with God, or get healed, or get delivered, we need to jump right into the Holy Ghost party. We need to rejoice with those whom God has set free. **"It's a Miracle!"**

## AIN'T NO PARTY LIKE A HOLY GHOST PARTY

In the meetings we have across America and around the world, at times, things get wild. What do I mean by this? When God shows up and shows off, He does things that you would never expect. When the power of God comes upon you, you might find yourself laughing, crying, shouting, etc. I've seen people do all kinds of things when they get healed, saved, delivered, and set free. It's glorious to be in the presence of God.

Not too long ago I was at a meeting when the power of God hit myself plus three other ladies. We found ourselves laughing and crying and holding onto one another.

When God shows up like that just go ahead and soak in His glory. These three ladies and I got drunk in the Holy Spirit. I mean, we were just wiped out, and we were just holding on to each other. We were in worship and just kind of rocking together.

Someone came up behind us and said something and all four of us just went down under the power of God. Some might not understand why people fall to the ground when the glory of God comes, but this is nothing new. It happened in the Old Covenant and the New Covenant.

*"So that the priests could not stand to minister because of the cloud: for the glory of the Lord had filled the house of the Lord." 1 Kings 8:11*

*"So that the priests could not stand to minister by reason of the cloud: for the glory of the Lord had filled the house of God." 2 Chronicles 5:14*

In the Book of John, when they came to arrest Jesus, He asked them who they were looking for. The minute Jesus answered them, the soldiers were hit with the power of God. They went backwards, and the Bible says they fell to the ground.

Now, that must have been rather dramatic, so why should we be surprised when the glory of God comes upon people, and they can no longer stand to their feet?

Even in the Old Covenant when people stood before kings, they had to fall on their faces. When Jesus comes into a meeting, He is the King of kings and Lord of lords, and when His presence becomes extremely strong, you will find yourself on the floor.

I couldn't get up off the floor. I tried. We were all trying to get off the floor because all four of us sometimes help on the ministry team, knowing that we needed to get up to help pray for people. One of the ladies was saying that we needed to get up off the floor.

I said, "I know, but how do we do that? We're stuck!"

One of the pastors walked up and said, "Oh, I'll help you."

I said to the girls, "Don't trust him, he's the reason we're on the floor. Don't let him touch you."

We found out later it wasn't him. It was the apostle of that church. But I kept blaming that pastor friend. I insisted he was the one who whispered in my ear and caused us to fall out. I said, "Don't let him help you."

One of the ladies said, "I'm getting up."

I said, "Well, tell us how you are going to do it, so we will all know how to get up."

She said, "Roll over and push up."

We all rolled over and tried to push up but seemed like we were stuck.

She said, "Okay roll back over and raise your right arm up."

We all rolled over and raised our right arm.

I said, "It's still not working we cannot get up."

She said, "Well, raise your leg up like this."

So, we all raised our legs in the air and I said, "Now what?"

She said, "I don't know." This caused us to laugh even harder and stay stuck to the floor.

When the Holy Spirit comes upon you in this way, at times you will get silly. You are not trying to be silly, but you just get silly. Now you might question, would God really do this? Absolutely! Remember He said we must become as little children to enter the kingdom of heaven. God also loves to humble us. It may make us look silly at times.

When the Holy Spirit comes upon me, sometimes I get wiped out and get kind of silly and crazy. I would rather have that than somebody sitting there like a bump on a log with no joy, no life, no excitement, and no hunger. The good news is that when God does this, you are not going to be hung over the next day.

Don't be a spectator. Just go ahead and jump in. I say, 'hold your nose and jump in by faith.' If I go swimming, I do not like to get water up my nose. That's why I hold my nose. Even if it is glory water, I just don't like water in my nose. So, I just hold my nose and run and jump. If the water bothers you in your nose, just hold your nose and run up and jump in.

I am always ready to rejoice. I'm not going to let you have all the fun all by yourself. I'm joining in. Sometimes we need that encounter or experience with the Lord. God's glory is awesome. His presence, and fire are so refreshing and fun, and I just thank Him for His refreshing.

---

**Psalm 85:6 *"Wilt thou not revive us again: that thy people may rejoice in thee?"***

---

It reminds me of the song that declares, *"Your goodness is running after; it's running after me."* Are you ready for him to run after you? God has been so good to us. I just want to say thank you Lord, for being so, so good to me.

When you worship Him and you jump in the water and you have fun, you bless Him. He's like, "Look at my kids having fun!" **It's Refreshing!**

## BUFORD DOWELL'S TESTIMONY ABOUT SUPERNATURALLY BEING ABLE TO PLAY THE ORGAN

Buford Dowell is a famous organist. How he ended up becoming an organist is an amazing story. It all began when my dad, Jack Coe Sr., prophesied over him and laid his hands upon him. As a young man Buford always wanted to play the organ.

Buford knew my father as a young boy and attended his church as one of the youths. When Buford was between twelve and fourteen years old my dad told him that he was going to be taking his regular organist with him on the road for tent meetings.

He told Buford, "You're going to have to stay behind at the church and play the organ for our church services."

Buford told him, "I would be glad to, but there's only one problem."

My dad said, "What's that, Buford?"

He said, "I don't know how to play the organ."

My dad said to him, "Well, you're always sitting over there by the organist."

He said, "Yes, sir. That is because I want to play the organ. I want to learn how to play. I love it, and I want to do it, but I don't know how to. That's why I'm sitting there hoping that maybe one day I could learn how to play."

My dad said, "That's your only problem is you don't know how to play?"

Buford said, "Yes sir, that's a pretty big one!"

When he said this, my dad told Buford, "That's no problem." Then he told him, "Give me your hands.

Buford said, "I extended out my hands towards Mr. Coe."

When Buford told me this story, he literally said to me, "Joanna let me tell you what God did through your dad's prayers. It is because of your dad's obedience to God that I can now play the organ."

Buford told me, "Your dad started to pray over my hands. This is what your dad said, 'God, let this boy play that Organ, piano, whatever he needs to play, just teach him right off and let him start playing immediately. Now, you know Lord that I need an organist, and I believe Buford is that man.'

Then he looked me in the eyes, and he told me with the most serious look I have ever seen, 'Okay, you're going to start playing the organ. Your first service will be next Sunday while I am out of town.' Then your dad simply turned around and walked away from me."

He said, "In my mind I am thinking, 'but I don't know how to play.'"

Buford had already taken a couple small lessons for playing the organ. He was told by the teacher that he would never be able to play the organ or the piano. The teacher told him, "The only thing you will ever be able to play is the radio."

Of course, this really shook him, and robbed him of his dream and his desire to play the organ. That is, until my dad prayed for him and prophesied over him.

Buford continued to tell me, "I am saying in my heart, 'What is wrong with brother Jack Coe? Has he lost his mind? Me? Play the organ?' At that very moment it was like the Lord tapped me on the shoulder and said, 'Son, you have seen the blind eyes open. You have seen the lame walk, the deaf healed. You have seen people come off hospital beds.

Those same hands that Jack Coe Sr. lays his hands on for people to receive their **Miracle**s, are the same hands he just laid upon you to play the organ.' The Lord said to me, 'You're going to play the organ.' At that very moment, I just said, 'Okay.'"

Now back in those days many people had organs and pianos in their homes. So, Buford went home, and he said to his mom, "Mom I'm going to play the organ."

She said, "That's nice." Of course, she did not take him seriously at all.

So, Buford, by faith, goes over to their organ and he begins to hit the keys with one finger. Over and over and over he kept pushing the keys. This was the very first day that he began to try to play.

The third day he sat down and just kept trying to play the organ with 1 to 2 fingers. He practiced all day, and it was getting annoying to those in the house.

On the fourth day he was now using three fingers. His mom was thinking to herself, 'Oh Lord, who told him that he could play the organ?'

By the fifth day he was using five fingers. He would not quit, because brother Jack Coe had laid his hands upon him, prophesying that he would play the organ. The Lord had spoken to his heart and confirmed that Brother Coe had heard from heaven.

On the sixth day something supernatural happened. Buford Dowell began to play the organ like a professional. His mother was overwhelmed with what just happened to her son. She began to run to all her neighbors and telling them, "Come to my house and hear my son play the organ." This was the beginning of the amazing career and life of Buford Dowell's ministry.

He began to play so professionally that he ended up playing not only for my dad, but for Kathryn Kuhlman. He played for William Branham, AA Allen, RW Schambach, and many more well-known evangelist and ministers. He also has traveled to over 58 nations of the world, ministering for Jesus Christ. **"It's a Miracle!"**

# LIVE OR DIE IN JESUS' NAME!

Buford Dowell ended up being in many of the tent meetings with my dad. Brother Buford said that there was one meeting that really stood out to him. It was when he was still a young man. Buford said he went out back and begin to count the ambulances. He said, "I do not know why I did, but I did." He said he counted 83 ambulances that were all lined up out back behind the huge tent.

He told me, "When I told your dad, he said to me, 'Oh, that's nice.' I knew your dad liked to put the people close to him that had six months or less to live. When the glory of God hit the place, your dad wanted to get his hands on these people immediately.

Buford said he still remembers that night. "Your dad was preaching with such authority and fire- when suddenly, the power of God was in that huge tent." He said, "The Holy Spirit was so strong on your dad. He was preaching a very strong and powerful message. It was powerful like the one your dad preached called, *God Will Set Your Fields on Fire*."

Buford continued to tell me, "Your dad went over to the black curtain. He had a big black curtain on the stage that went all the way across the platform, with a big American flag on it. Now, behind that curtain would be those who had six months or less to live. All these people were on stretchers, cots, and hospital beds. Some of them had their doctors right there with them and their nurses.

They had friends, family, nurses, and other caregivers there just trying to help keep them alive. Some of these people were hooked up to medical devices because they could die at any moment. Your dad went over to this curtain between them and the crowd. He grabbed that big black curtain, and he started pulling it open across the platform. Then he went over to the people lying in the hospital beds, the cots, and the stretchers.

He began to grab these people, and he started throwing them out of their beds, and off their cots, and stretchers. I mean, he was grabbing them and throwing them into the air. While he was doing this he was shouting, **'Live or Die in Jesus' name!'** Every person he was grabbing, he was shouting, **'Live or Die, in Jesus' Name!'** Over and over, he was shouting, 'In Jesus Name, Live or Die,' as he was throwing the people off the stretchers, the cots, and hospital beds."

Buford said, "As he was doing this, the doctors, nurses, friends, and family members were screaming, 'You're killing them! You're killing them!' Or yelling, 'What do you think you are doing?' Some of these people that Jack had thrown onto the ground were just lying on the ground flopping like fish out of the water. They looked like they were going to die at any minute!"

He said, "While all of this was happening, an even greater wave of God's glory hit the tent. Some of these people that Jack had thrown into the air were instantly healed. They started running, leaping, and jumping. Some of them began to jump up and spin like tops, faster than a human possibly could spin. The glory of God got so strong that some of the people who were still in their cots and hospital beds began to jump up out of them.

Medical equipment and IVs were going everywhere, with doctors and nurses almost losing their minds. It was divine mayhem. I didn't know what to do. The power of God was hitting the whole crowd in the tent.

Thousands of people were jumping up and down and running all through the tent. Some of them were climbing the tent poles going up and down. Some of these people were going up the tent poles so fast that they looked like a rocket taking off. People were on the tent poles everywhere doing supernatural acrobatics, flipping, and turning, and spinning. He said it was better than any circus he had ever gone to in his life."

He said, "The place was wild, and yet at the same time, people were running to the altars. People were giving their hearts to God. People were getting saved. People were getting delivered. Demons were screaming and coming out of people, and Holy

Spirit joy filled the place. Holy Ghost fire was all over the place. God's glory filled the place. This all began because a man heard from God. He obeyed God and began to throw the people out of their deathbeds, declaring, 'Live or Die, in Jesus Name!'"

It is time for you to decide what you want to do! Live or die, in Jesus Name!

Buford said that when it came time to go home, only one person got into an ambulance out of the 83 ambulances he had counted earlier. He said, "I don't know if they got in the ambulance because they needed a ride home, or they were the only one who did not get healed. Most of the time, when people got healed, the ambulance didn't take them home, but this person may not have had somebody there." He didn't know the whole situation regarding this one person, but what he did know was, **"It's a Miracle!"**.

# CHAPTER THREE

## NO MORE CRUTCHES FOR HIM

The Holy Spirit had moved upon my dad into a place of extreme seriousness. He was not going to play around with the sickness and the disease. It seems as if most Christians do not realize that it is the devil that is attacking them. We need to wake up and realize that God knows there is a devil who is tormenting you.

God wants you healed. God wants to set you free. Jesus Christ, the Son of God, took your place. He took your sickness, your disease and your torment and placed it on the cross. He did it to save your soul and set you free from the power of the devil.

There are ministers too busy playing patty-cake in the church, trying to appease people. Sometimes we might need to just get a little radical. I don't go around kicking and hitting people. I don't go around jerking them out of wheelchairs… yet. I've come close. At times my husband has said to me, "You are beginning to act like your dad."

I remember in one service the Holy Spirit led me to go over to a man who was sitting in the congregation. He was sitting in the second row, and I went over to him, and I said, "You know, Jesus says arise, take up your bed and walk." I did not even ask him, 'Do you want to get up?' I just grabbed his hand, and I jerked him up out of his chair.

I told him, "It's time for you people to be healed." I was just using him as an example not realizing that he was crippled. I grabbed his arm and I jerked him up in the air and I said, "Let's go, let's show them."

That's when you get healed, when by faith, you walk, you run, and you leap. You get excited.

Just as I was saying, "Come on," I looked down and discovered that there were crutches on the floor.

The devil whispered in my ear, "You have done it now. You just pulled a crippled man up out of his chair. What are you going to do now?" There was a little bit of fight that was going on inside of me during this time because the devil was saying, "You're going to embarrass yourself."

Well, you know what? I'm not the healer. I do not really care if I embarrass myself. I'm here to see people get set free. I'm here to see people get healed because I know the One who does it. His name is Jesus.

Before I knew it, I had that man grabbed by the arm. It took him a while to get up. I said, "Come on, come on, come on!"

I started to make him run with me. I told him, "Come on, you are slowing us down!" Finally, I let him get back to his seat and I went back to preaching.

At the end of this service my husband was trying to get my attention. "Honey," he said, "look there at the man you took a hold of."

I thought he was going to criticize me, so I told him, "I know, the devil has already told me what I did."

I looked over and I saw him over at his chair. He was standing up and holding onto the chair and moving his leg back and forth. I thought, 'Oh no, I have hurt that man! He's trying to get his leg straightened out. Oh God, I'm so sorry!'

I went running over to him and asked him, "Are you okay? Are you okay?"

He said, "Oh yeah, I'm just showing my wife. Look, look, I can do this! Look, look, look at my legs! Look at what the Lord has done!"

God had completely healed him. The Lord had made his legs whole. I simply picked him out of the crowd to use as an example without having any idea that he had a problem with his legs.

We baby sit that devil way too much. Doctor Jesus says it's time for you to believe it and receive it. Every word in this Bible is true. If God is a liar, then let us go home and just forget it. But I am here to tell you that God is not a liar. He says what He means, and He means what He says. We know what a liar does. He just keeps on lying.

In all the years that I have known Jesus Christ, He has never lied about one thing to me. It is time for us to take him at his word. It's time for you to believe the word of God. Some of you have been getting in healing line, after healing line, after healing line, and nothing's happening. It's time for you to believe God and put the devil in his place. **"It's a Miracle!"**

# JACK COE HEALED OF MALARIA

When my dad was a young man, God called him to go in the army. While he was serving in the army, he contracted tropical malaria because of some treatments the army doctors gave him. Gradually he grew worse, and the army had transferred him to Le Garde General Hospital, in New Orleans, Louisiana. He sought God to heal him of this affliction that was gradually taking his life.

The malarial chills kept coming more frequent and his body becoming weaker. They decided to transfer him to Harmon General Hospital at

Longview, Texas. At the Harmon hospital the chills and fever were more acute, and at times, he would go out of his mind. For fifty-four hours he ran temperatures of over 106°. His spleen and liver swelled until it was twice their normal size. He would lay in bed biting his tongue until it bled because of the pain.

The army doctor told my dad, "Soldier, I've got bad news for you. We've done all that medical science can do. You have one of the worst cases of tropical malaria that has ever come to this hospital. We've tried every kind of medicine that we have on hand, but you are not getting any better. Due to the condition of the spine, along with other ailments, you don't have long to live. Do you want to spend the rest of your time in the army, or do you want to go home to your wife and family?"

Finally, the fever broke, and he was feeling better, and He told the doctor he wanted to go home with his family.

The major told him they would get his papers for medical discharge. He said, "I don't want to frighten you, but if you have one more attack like the one you just went through, you will die."

Well, my dad came home from the army, and he continued as a traveling evangelist. In one of his revival meetings, he got extremely sick. He remembered that the doctors told him if he had malaria again, he would die. He started running a 104° fever. Then his temperature climbed to 105°.

The next day 105.6°. and on the fourth day,106° to 106.7°. He got so delirious that he could not preach.

He told my mom, "Honey you are going to have to go do the meeting."

She said, "What do you want me to do?"

He said, "You know what to do. Just sing and preach. Do whatever you need to do. "

He laid in the bed, and he said, "God, I do not want to leave my wife and baby now. You've got to help me some way, somehow, anyway You can: live or die, sink or swim I'm either going to get healed or I'm coming to you!"

As he laid in that bed of death he went through the Bible. He was so sick that he could hardly hold his head up. As he was laying in that bed and reading the Bible, faith began to rise in his heart.

He told the Lord, "This is your Word." Then he began to search his heart and said, "Lord, reveal anything in my heart that ought not to be there."

The Lord said, "What about the people you talked about? Remember the offering I gave you last week and you grumbled about it?"

There were numerous things that came to him, and he begin to cry out to God to forgive him and ask Him to put it under the blood.

Then he raised his hands toward heaven and said,

"Either you're going to let me die and take me home; or you're going to raise me up. If you called me to preach, then I am not going to lay in some bed sick. I'm not going to lay in some bed disabled. I'm not going to continue to take this pain and sickness. I want this out of my body. And You said **You are the Lord that healeth me**! You are the Lord my healer, and I am going to take You at Your Word!"

Suddenly, a supernatural light came from the corner of the room. It kept coming toward him, getting brighter and brighter and bigger. Then it hovered over the top of his bed, and over the top of him. It was so bright. He said it felt as if someone poured a bucket of oil over his head and went all way down to his feet. He got up out of the bed and he knew he was healed.

The symptoms of malaria tried to come back a few days later, because the devil will try to come back. So, my dad got a fever again and he climbed into bed.

God said, "Jack, what are you doing in bed?"

He said, "Well, I'm sick, God. I have a 104° fever again and chills."

God said, "Jack, did I not heal you?"

And Jack said, "Yes."

God said, "Then get out of that bed."

At that moment my daddy agreed with God. "That's right, I'm not sick." And he got up.

Then the Lord told him, "Now, Jack, because you listened to that devil, and you believed that you got malaria back after I already healed you, I want you to get your Bible and go out on the street corner and preach."

He said, "I had to go be a street corner preacher. I used to make fun of them, but because I listened to that stupid devil, now I have to go be a street corner preacher. While I was out on the streets people were saved, healed, and delivered. And that malaria never came back." **"It's a Miracle!"**

## HEALING IS THE CHILDREN'S BREAD

We need to understand that sicknesses, diseases, and all that is evil, are the consequences of living in a fallen world. Divine healing is when faith in Jesus and the Holy Spirit come together. There is a response from Heaven. There is a movement of God.

There is a manifestation of the Spirit and a divine explosion, caused by faith in God. Divine healing is a result of believing that Jesus Christ is the same yesterday, today and forever. It is believing and accepting the provisions that Jesus made in the atonement for healing of our physical bodies.

Remember, when Jesus shows up it's natural for Him to heal and deliver people. Jesus doesn't say, "I'll be right back. I left it at home." No, He says, "Arise, take up your bed and walk."

There are times healing is immediately or suddenly. Other times it is a process. There are times we do not see the manifestation of healing at the meeting. But then they contact us and relay to us the amazing stories of what God did after we left. There are many ways that my God heals. He is still on the throne, and He still heals today.

## THE MAN WITHOUT EYEBALLS

I was headed to Tennessee to get ready for a set of meetings. I had just flown in from Corpus Christi, Texas, where I had been conducting meetings the previous week. I just got to the airport in Nashville when my phone rang. The man on the other end said, "I know you don't know me, but I understand you are Jack Coe Sr.'s daughter."

I said, "Yes, I am."

He said, "I must tell you a story about your dad. I was about 18 years old, and I was at one of your dad's tent meetings. As a young man I had been telling pastors, preachers, and different people that I knew that I was called to preach. All these ministers and people would just pacify me by patting me on the head and they would say things like, 'That's nice young man.'

But nobody would recognize I had a call upon my life to preach. Now, their attitudes were really burning me up. I really did not know what to do because nobody was encouraging me, and I knew in my heart that I was called to preach. I heard about your dad holding a tent meeting. I went to this meeting with great excitement and expectation because of all of the amazing **Miracle**s I had heard that were transpiring."

This man continued saying, "So, I found myself sitting there in your dad's tent when suddenly your dad stopped preaching and pointed right back at me. He said, 'Young man, you, right there.'

I said, 'Me?'

He said, 'Yes, you, stand up! Young man, you are called to preach. Come on up here.'

In my mind I said, 'Wow, he's going to let me preach.' I was so excited.

I got up beside him on the stage. And he said, 'Now I know you are called to preach, but this is my tent. I'm going to ask you to help me tonight, but you're not going to preach in my tent tonight. If you want to preach, then believe God to get your own tent.'"

That is just how my dad was sometimes. He was very straightforward and blunt. He meant what he said, and he said what he meant. But he said to this young man, "Tonight, I want you to help me and go with people as they are getting healed."

This man said, "Your dad told me, 'There will be times when people will take off running. I even tell them to start running. But when they do, I want you to run with them. And as you are running at their side, I want you to tell them, 'Jack Coe, doesn't do this, Jesus Christ does this.'

He started praying for the people. The ones that needed healing in their legs or parts of their bodies when he got done praying for them, he would tell them to run. That was my cue. They would take off running and I'd run beside them. That is when I would begin to boldly proclaim in their ear as they ran, **'Jack Coe doesn't do this; Jesus Christ does this! Jack Coe doesn't do this; Jesus Christ does this!'**

As the people were coming down the prayer line, I could see that a lady was coming with a man who seemed to be blind. Your dad then announced, 'Ladies and gentlemen, a blind man is coming. How many of you believe God can open the eyes of the blind?'

They all begin to cheer and shout, 'YES!'

Jack said, 'God's going to open this blind man's eyes.' The whole place just kept cheering and yelling and shouting and praising God. When this blind man finally reached him, brother Coe just kept talking to the people. He reached his hands towards the man, and with his thumbs, he took hold of the man's eyelids. He pulled up the man's eyelids with his thumbs. He never even looked into the man's face, but he kept telling the people, 'God is good, and He will do what He has done in the past, now. Jesus still opens the eyes of the blind.'

During this time, I was trying to get brother Coe's attention. I could see over brother Coe's shoulder, and I noticed that the man had no eyeballs. Brother Jack was looking out at the large gathering of people, so he was not looking into the man's face. I am trying to tell him, 'The man has no eyeballs!' And he is telling all the people who are there that this man is going to see.

I was trying to save his reputation and his ministry. But no matter how I kept trying to interrupt what he was saying, he just kept talking. He finally gave me a look and said, 'Go get your own tent.'

After brother Coe was done encouraging the people to believe, he said, 'Alright everybody, stretch out your hands this way, close your eyes, and we're going to pray.'

He now had his hands over the empty sockets on this man's face, where his eyeballs should have been. Brother Coe put his hands over this blind man's empty eye sockets. He is praying, 'In the name of Jesus, let this man's eyes be open to see.'

I'm thinking, 'What do you mean? He has no eyeballs. How could they be open? There are no eyeballs in that man's head!'

When brother Coe was done praying, he stepped back away from the man. Once again, with divine boldness, he said, 'In the name of Jesus eyes be open!' Then brother Coe once again stepped towards the blind man and grabbed the man's eyelids, pulling them up.

When he lifted this man's eyelids, I could clearly see into the man's skull. I thought, "knew it, I knew it, I knew he had no eyeballs.' I was going to get more radical with brother Coe because he would not listen. But just as I was fixing to become forceful, I saw two brown eyes beginning to form in this man's eye sockets. It started as two tiny dots, one in each eye.

Then, these tiny dots began to make circles and kept spinning around. It is hard to explain what I saw happening. A creative **Miracle** was happening before my very own eyes in this man's eye sockets. I saw white and I saw brown. And then I saw these things coming together. Suddenly the man had two beautiful brown eyes.

I was so overwhelmed with what I saw that at that very moment, I took off running. At the top of my lungs, I was shouting, 'Come see the man who had no eyeballs, that now has eyeballs! Come see the man who had no eyeballs that now has eyeballs!

Come see the man who had no eyeballs that now has eyeballs!'

I was so excited that I ran out of the tent. Next thing you know, I was about a quarter of a mile away from the tent and I was still shouting, 'Come see the man who had no eyeballs and now has eyeballs!' When I realized that I was not even in the tent I thought, 'Oh, I better get back.' As I was running back towards the tent, I was shouting, 'Come see the man who had no eyeballs, and now he's got eyeballs!'

When I got back into the tent, your dad said to me, 'Young man, where have you been?' I tried to tell brother Coe, but brother Coe said, 'We do not have time to talk and visit right now, we have lots of people to pray for here. Get up here on the stage I need your help.'

As we were talking, here came a man in a wheelchair. His one foot was almost facing backwards. And his one leg was only half the size of the other leg. Brother Coe said to the large crowd in the tent, 'God's going to bring this leg out and straighten up his foot. How many of you will believe with me for this **Miracle** from God?' Of course, the whole multitude roared that they believed with him. They had just seen a man with no eyeballs get a new set of eyeballs.

Brother Coe reached his hands out to this man's small, shriveled up leg. He's got his hands around his leg and suddenly that leg began to grow out. This leg in comparison to the good leg was only about half its size. But I watched as this leg grew out to become a normal leg like the other one.

Then my heart almost stopped beating as I saw that one foot, which was turned around facing backwards, begin to spin. I am telling you that it did not just turn, but it spun. I had to rub my eyeballs because I could not believe what I was seeing. When it was done spinning, it was facing forward. The foot was just as normal as the other foot. Brother Coe told me to run. I think he wanted me to run with the man with the new leg, but I was beside myself.

I took off running and shouting as I ran, 'Come see the man that had his foot turned around and half of a leg grew out! Come see the man that had his foot turned around and half of a leg grew out! Come see the man that had his foot turned around and half of a leg grew out!' Before I realized what I was doing I had gone a quarter of a mile outside of the tent.

My life was never the same from that day forward. I went into the ministry. Before I left your dad's tent, he turned to me and said, 'You are going to see amazing **Miracle**s in your life and ministry. You will see **Miracle**s because God is in you, and He will begin to use you.' From that day till now I have gone many places and seen many **Miracle**s just like your dad prophesied. But I need to tell you that I have never seen the **Miracle**s like I saw in your dad's ministry."

You see, God wants to use us. He wants to do **Miracle**s because He doesn't want people to be sick, lame, halt, or with any disease. He wants to see people saved. That's why Jesus died. The devil is a bully and God does not want you bullied and tormented. He is the Lord, your healer. **"It's a Miracle!"**

# THE BLIND MAN RECEIVES SIGHT

I was sitting in my hotel in Long Island, New York, and my phone rang. It was the pastor of the church where I was getting ready to go preach that night.

The pastor said, "I'm sorry, I'm late picking you up, but I am on my way. I just wanted you to know that I'm going to be picking up a blind man. And when you get to church tonight, you're going to pray for him. And God's going to open his eyes."

I said, "Hallelujah, praise the Lord! Yes! That's so awesome! Amen!"

In many churches and places, I go, I'm always saying to bring the blind, bring the lame, bring the sick, bring the busted, disgusted, the possessed, and oppressed, and God will heal them. I remember hearing my dad say that many times, so I thought, 'yeah, go ahead and bring the blind, bring the lame, bring the deaf, bring the sick and diseased,' but now somebody had taken me up on my word and was bringing them.

I hung up with the pastor, I went, "Oh God, oh God, the pastor's bringing a blind man and she says that I'm going to pray for him and You're going to heal him! Oh God, they are expecting a **Miracle**!"

Now many times I say that expectation breeds **Miracle**s, but I think I had lost my own expectation because of fear. 'Oh no!' I thought, 'what if God doesn't heal him? Oh no! The pastor says that this blind man is coming and God's going to open his blind eyes. Oh, what if He doesn't?'

This pastor picked me up and she was telling me how she dropped the blind man off at the church and he was all excited. And I'm acting like this is so great. But on the inside, I'm like, 'Oh God, please! You must show up! Oh God, you must be there!'

So we get to the church service. My message for that night was about the blind man on the road to Jericho out of Luke 18:35-43. I had not planned on this being the message, but this is what the Lord laid upon my heart. He was the man who cried out, "Jesus, thou son of David have mercy on me."

I told the congregation, "Jesus said to the blind man, what will you have me to do?"

And the blind man said, "Lord, that I may receive my sight."

Jesus said, **"Receive your sight. Your faith has made thee whole."**

I was all excited and pumped-up preaching about this blind man and the blind man receiving his sight. I had completely forgotten about the blind man in this church service.

I invited all the people to come on down for prayer, no matter what was wrong. Just as I was telling all the people to come, I saw out of my left eye the blind man. They were bringing the blind man to be prayed for. I said, "Lord, there's the blind man over there. They're bringing him up here."

And just to show you how much faith I have, I went in the opposite direction. The blind man was to my left. I went to the middle of the people in the line and headed to my right. Then the next one, and the next one, and the next one. I would glance out of my left eye and say, "Jesus, the blind man is over there on my left." I found myself trying to avoid the blind man.

Then I heard the voice of the Lord and He said to me, "What are you doing?"
I said, "You know, I'm working it up."

God said, "What are you working up?"

I said, "Well, you know."

He said, "No, I don't know. Tell me what you're working up."

I said, "Faith. Some of these people are getting healed. I'm working up faith."

And He said, "Well, let me know when you get it worked up." And then the Lord said to me, "Do you know that your dad had a situation similar to this once. He said, bring the blind, the lame and all of those that are sick. He boldly proclaimed God would heal them."

The Lord reminded me right then of the story about my father. One night they brought a blind lady to the church where my dad was preaching.

The pastor of that church said, "Brother Coe, I hope you're hearing from God, because what if the people don't get healed?"

And my dad said, "Well, what if they do?"

The pastor of that church said, "Yeah, but what if they don't, then what about my reputation? What about my church?"

My dad said, "What if they do? Then what will happen to your reputation and your church?"

Well, at that night service, people came with headaches and backaches, and they were getting healed. But about halfway up the prayer line came this blind lady. When she reached my dad he said, "Ma'am you are going to have to go to the back of the prayer line." And so, they helped her go back to the end of the prayer line.

During that whole prayer time my dad kept saying to God, "Lord the blind lady is getting closer. God, the blind lady's getting closer."

God said to my father, "Jack, you do your part, and I'll do mine." He prayed for her, and God opened her eyes to see.

The minute I remembered that story it hit me. That is when the Lord said to me, "Joanna, you do your part, and I will do mine."

Divine boldness hit me, and I went right over to the blind man to pray for him. He was sitting over in a pew on my far left, and I went over, and I said, "I'm going to pray for your eyes. Do you believe God can open them?"

And he said, "I don't know."

I said, "Well, I do. The blind man on the road to Jericho received his sight and you can receive yours!"

God told me to do my part and He would do His. So I put my thumbs on his eyes and I began to pray. I remember my husband praying for people in Dunn, North Carolina, and in different places. He would put his thumbs on their eyes and people would start to see. So, I thought maybe the thumbs work, you know, sometimes we kind of follow suit with what other people are doing. Thank God, that in our ignorance, He still uses us.

So, I put my thumbs on this man's eyes and I begin to pray. And while I'm praying, out of my mouth came these words, "You're going to begin to see light. And the light is going to get so bright that it's going to hurt. It's going to give you a headache. When this begins to happen, you say, 'I want to see, I want to receive my sight.' Begin to ask to receive your sight.

The next thing that is going to happen is that you are going to see dark forms and movements. Then you're going to realize these dark forms will take shape. Then you will realize that it may be people, or it may be a dresser, or it may be something else. You are not going to be quite sure of what it is that you are seeing, but you will know it is a dark form, and you will know that it has a shape to it. Then you will begin to experience colors. After all of this you will begin to see more clearly. Your eyes will become so clear that you will be able to read. You will be able to distinguish between different things, and your eyes will be completely restored."

As these words were coming out of my mouth I was thinking, 'Oh, my goodness, what is it that I just said?' This is how God works at times. There are many biblical examples of this throughout the Scriptures.

After I was done speaking these words
and praying, I said, "Okay, what do you see?"

He said, "Nothing."

Well, you know, there was a blind man in the Book
of Mark that Jesus prayed for more than once, so I
figured that I could pray more than once as well.
When I was done praying for him again, it didn't
seem like anything happened, but remember the
Bible says to lay hands on the sick and they shall
recover.

People seem to lose their faith when you pray for
them, and nothing happens right away. But
something *is* happening, and something *is* taking
place. The Holy Spirit is working within their body.

Remember, I did not say that he would have results
right away. I told him that within a few days these
different things would happen and then he would
receive his sight. So, I put my thumbs back on his
eyes and prayed again. I asked him again, "What
are you seeing?"

Again, he said, "Nothing."

I said to him, "Okay, well you just sit right here, and
I'll check back."

I told the Lord, "God, you know we are not letting
go. We believe Your Word, and we believe
you, God."

I went on praying for other people. I said to myself, 'Well you know, God did say in a few days, so you just hold on to faith.'

I got to the hotel that night and the devil said, "You know why you said what you did? Because you are a traveling evangelist, and in a few days, you will be gone from this town. You can say whatever you want to if you push it into the future."

When the devil said this to me, I said to the Lord, "I'm not like that! Oh God, I wouldn't do that! You know, God, I wouldn't do that! I tell people the truth. I didn't even expect to say those things to that blind man!" The enemy tortured me all night long. I could not get any peace that night and I kept saying, "Oh God, forgive me! Was I wrong with what I said?"

We need to realize that the devil fights **Miracle**s tooth and nail because when God performs **Miracle**s, it's a sledgehammer blow against all his lies. **Miracle**s from God come against everything the enemy has been lying about.

The next night as I am getting ready for church, the phone rings. It's the pastor again and she says, "I'm sorry, but I'm running late again. I'm going by to pick up the blind man. By the way, he is seeing bright lights and his head is hurting him just like you said it would. He thinks that there is a nightlight in his room, but he's not quite sure. He is also seeing a little movement of a dark form. He knows that you told him these things would happen. He would like for you to pray for him again so he can receive the completion of his sight."

I said, "Awesome!" And I hung up the phone.

When the pastor told me these things, I was very encouraged. I realized that the devil had been lying to me all night, but I also thought, 'Oh no! They are bringing the blind man again! Oh God, you have got to be there!'

The pastor finally arrived to pick me up. We got into the car and the pastor was really excited. What I had prophesied was beginning to come to pass for this blind man. That night I ministered what God had laid upon my heart, and to be honest with you, I don't even remember what I preached.

During this whole service I kept thinking, 'The blind man is back.' I remembered how the enemy fought me all night long. I told God, "I don't want to tell nothing but the truth."

The Lord said to me, "You did. That's why I'm letting you know. Instead of in a few days, I have already let him begin to see light and forms of dark things moving." And sure enough, that's what He was doing.

But when we called everyone up for prayer, here they come bringing the blind man and set him in the pew on my far left. So, I started in the middle and went right again, thinking, 'Oh there's the blind man.'

After I prayed for some more people on my right side, God said, "Are you working it up again?"

I said, "No Sir, I'm just afraid he won't get healed."

God told me, "You're not the healer, I am. Take the pressure off yourself and go pray for the blind man."

Then I immediately went over to this blind man. I found out his name was Eddie. I said, "Hi, Eddie, nice to see you. I'm glad you're back. I understand you might be seeing bright lights?"

He said, "Oh yeah, I think there's a picture of Jesus in my room. I think I saw it for a moment, either that, or he appeared in my room. And there is this nightlight by my bed. It is the first light I saw. Then some other lights got brighter in the hall and different things, but I'm not quite sure of everything yet."

So, I began to pray for God to open his eyes and I am believing we were going to see it happen. Everybody in the church was going to see it. Then I said, "Well, Eddie, what do you see?"

He said, "Nothing!"

I said, "Okay, we'll keep praying and believing God. Do you know that God is doing it?"

He responded, "Yes, I do. And I want to see. I especially want to see that picture of Jesus in my room." He started telling me a whole list of all of the things that he really desired to see with his physical eyes.

I said to Eddie, "Well, is there anything else you want me to pray for?"

"Well," he said, "yeah, I want you to pray for my friend Ginger." I notice there is a lady standing with her walker right next to him that he invited to church. She had sugar diabetes, and it was causing her to go blind. Her kidneys were bad, and all kinds of other things were wrong with her.

I turned to pray for her, and I said, "Ginger, may I pray for your eyes too?"

She told me that I could. As I was praying for her, I remember just kind of hugging her and rubbing my hand up and down her back. She had on a red coat, and I was just loving on her, and just telling her that it was okay, and that God loved her. I knew that she had a lot of hurts in her life, so I was telling this to her and ministering inner healing as well as praying for her physical healing. As I am doing this, suddenly Eddie says, "I see red!"

I said, "What did you say?"

He said, "I see red. I see a hand moving, and I see red."

I said, "Eddie, that's your friend, Ginger's coat. And that's my hand that is moving up and down her back."

He said, "I see it!" Then he turned and he looked at the banners on the wall and he began to see these banners. These banners were covered with the different names of Jehovah. He also identified the banner that declares: *Jesus Is Lord.* Suddenly he turned and started reading these banners out loud. At that moment I got so excited that I just took off running throughout the sanctuary.

It was like the story that man told me about my father when he prayed for a man with no eyeballs. When God created those eyeballs, this young man took off running everywhere. When I came back to where Eddie was sitting the pastor said that he had suddenly lost his vision.

He began to say, "I can't see, I can't see."

I said, "What!?"

The pastor looked over and there was a man in a black suit standing in front of a banner, blocking Eddie's view. She told him to please move.

Eddie said, "Oh, now I can see!"

The enemy will do anything he can to rob you of what God has done for you.

On the way home that night Eddie saw the stop sign. He began to see things and he began to do things for his sister. Here is the shocking information that I have not yet shared, he was almost ninety years old. Age does not matter to God.

The next morning while Eddie and his sister was eating breakfast Eddie said, "Oh Sis! What happened to your hair!?" She had forgotten that he could see now, and she had come to breakfast without her wig and make-up on.

Eddie's sister, who was in her nineties, got mad at him for making fun of her hair so she gave him a list of chores to do. She told him, "Well, Eddie, now that you can see, you can get on the roof and fix it. And you can replace the shingles that blew off. And while you are at it you can scrub this kitchen floor."

I didn't think that was right. I thought he was too old to be doing that kind of stuff. When I heard this, I went over to him the next time saw him at the service and told him, "I heard you had to mop floors and that you had to pick up shingles that were blown off your house. I heard your sister made you work."

He said, "Yes."

I said, "I'm so sorry. I didn't mean for you to have to go right to work."

He said, "No, I'm so glad I can see that I'll do whatever they want me to do." He asked me, "Is there something I can do for you?"

I said, "Well, I live in Texas, but thank you anyways."

God is gracious and He is good, and He still opens the eyes of the blind. **"It's a Miracle!"**.

# CHAPTER FOUR
## OUR FIRST MIRACLE CRUSADE

I was in Corpus Christi, Texas, and several churches had come together for a healing crusade. Pastor Steve and Debbie, who were helping put this together, said to me, "You know, sister Joanna, we've never really had a healing meeting, or any healing evangelists come to the city of Corpus Christi for the main purpose of a healing crusade."

I said, "I'm sure people have come and done revival meetings, and they have been at churches."

They told me, "That is true, but there has never been a large gathering of churches supporting a healing service." They asked me if they could pull something together, would we be willing to come to minister? I told them that Randy and I would be happy to do the crusade.

These pastors got quite a few churches together and they went and rented the Selena auditorium in Corpus Christi, which was right next to the ocean.

Once we agreed to do this meeting, and everything was set up, I began thinking about how it all was going to work. Up until this point, we had never conducted a healing crusade. I didn't tell them that though. I'm supposed to be Jack Coe's daughter. My dad had humongous meetings where there were amazing healings, **Miracle**s, signs, and wonders. I sure didn't want it to look like I didn't know what to do.

They informed us that they were going to have a few smaller meetings in their storefront church before the crusade so we could discuss with the other pastors and leaders on what to do. They were leaning upon us heavily to make this work.

During the meetings I told them, "Well, we're going to pray for people, so we will need catchers. You need to get people to be catchers and train them how to catch."

One pastor spoke up and said, "Well, we catch people at our church. If you want me to, I'll be the one to train the catchers and we'll have a meeting on that."

I said, "Good deal."

So, they asked me, "What else do we do?"

I told them, "Well, we're going to need tissues and cloths to cover the people if they fall out. We also need a team of intercessors who will be praying before and during the meeting." I also told them, "I'm sure if a lot of people show up like you're telling me, Randy and I won't be able to get to them all so some of you pastors are going to have to help us pray for all of these people."

They said to me, "Well, what if nobody gets healed?"

I told them, "But what if they do?"

I told them a story that Papa Doorn once told me about my dad. Papa Doorn said, "Your dad said, 'You people are all looking to Jack Coe, but Jack Coe is not the healer. Jesus is the healer. To show you it is not Jack Coe, I'm going to pray over these college students, and they are the ones who are going to pray for you.' Jack laid hands on each of the students and said, 'Now you go pray for the people.' The people who were on crutches, in wheelchairs, and who were sick, all got in different lines."

One boy said, "I thought, 'oh good this lady coming doesn't look too bad.' But then she lifted up her blouse and there was a huge tumor."

The boy told the woman, "Lady what do you want me to do with that?"

She said, "Lay hands on it and pray for it to go."

The boy said, "I can't do that."

She said, "Oh yes you can because brother Coe said you could through Jesus Christ. Now lay your hands on me or else."

The boy said, "I didn't know if I was more scared of her or the tumor, but I laid hands on the tumor and prayed, and it just disappeared. I was so excited and so ready after that I said, 'Next!'"

Randy and I just laid hands on the pastors and begin to pray impartation for them to be able to pray for people so they would be healed. I was simply walking by faith into this project. All I knew was that we're going to this great big auditorium and there were going to be a whole lot of churches coming together and they were expecting great **Miracle**s. I was asking Jesus to please show up.

When we got the auditorium, we had another meeting with the catchers and pastors in a side room to answer questions, discuss the order of the service, and pray for **Miracle**s and healings. We had several different meetings, and they were looking to Randy and I, who had never done this before. We didn't want to act like we hadn't, but we didn't want to mislead people and tell them wrong either, so I would say, "Holy Spirit, help me, what do we do here? How do we do this?"

In one of those meetings, I said, "Well, you know, I remember in my dad's tent, He took up the offerings in Colonel Sanders fried chicken buckets. So, someone from one of the churches went to Kentucky Fried Chicken and got a bunch of fried chicken buckets for the offerings, just like my dad used to.

What is amazing is that right next to where we were holding these meetings is where the Ringling Brothers were setting up to do their circus. I had a flashback at that moment to the day my dad decided to have the largest tent in the world. It all came about when he looked out and he saw the Ringling Brother's tent.

He said, "If the devil can get a big crowd, then God, you can get a bigger crowd." Right then and there he went over to the Ringling Brother's tent and talked with some of their tent overseers to get its measurements. Then he went to the tent makers and told them, "Make me a tent bigger than this one." And that's when my dad's tent became the largest tent in the world.

Now I was standing on this massive platform. I was thinking back to when my dad had a black curtain on the platform that separated those who were terminally ill, from the rest of the congregation. My dad had these massive platforms where he had up to three hundred preachers sitting on the platform at one time.

And behind them was this black curtain where the extremely sick people waited to receive prayer. Now, we did not have enough room on this platform to do like my daddy did, but as I was remembering what had happened in his tent this reality hit me; there's no way I would ever fill my dad's shoes.

You see, all we must do is what God tells us to do. Sometimes we are too busy trying to fill someone else's shoes when all we need to do is get in the shoes of Jesus and follow Him. When the Lord gave me this revelation all the pressure lifted off me.

It was still exciting to stand on this platform in this big auditorium. It was exciting to see the Kentucky Fried Chicken buckets and knowing that the Ringling Brothers were going to be right next door. And then it was even more exciting to know that all these preachers were bringing their congregations to this gathering. People were going to be coming in wheelchairs and with walkers and on crutches who were expecting a **Miracle**.

This large auditorium we were in did not have good aisles and they did not have a good place up front to pray for the people. It had a concert area in the front that sunk down into the floor and lifted during performances. This had to be put down in the floor to have enough room at the altar to pray for everyone.

I began to line up different pastors who would pray for the people after I was done ministering the Word. I told the pastors, "I am not the only one who is going to pray for the sick and the needy. You are going to have to help me."

The services began, and we had a lot of people who needed healing. I told those in the meeting, "I can't get to all of you, but all these people who are on the ministry team have been fasting and praying. We have laid hands upon them for impartation. They are willing and ready to pray for you to believe God for your **Miracle**. I need you all to get in the prayer lines that we have formed if you need a **Miracle**. As you are waiting to be prayed for, be watching what God is doing up front because you will begin to see **Miracle**s happen in the different lines."

We began praying for people, and everybody had their lines. **Miracle**s were happening all over the auditorium. People were being healed. Headaches, ankles, knees, and backs were being healed as well. People were reporting stories for days after this meeting, but there was one that stood out to me.

There was one pastor there who would go down these prayer lines and every time he saw what he considered a very tough case he would grab ahold of them and begin to cut across everyone's line saying, "Excuse me, excuse me. This is an emergency. Excuse me. This one's serious. Excuse me." He would get them over to me and have me pray for that person.

In one situation he said, "Sister Joanna, you got to pray for this one."

I said, "What's wrong?"

He said, "This boy is blind in one eye. He can't see out of this side. You need to pray for him."

Immediately I remembered what happened in Hagerstown with that little girl and I said, "Yes God, you can do this."

So, I laid my hands on him and I covered up his good eye. I wanted to make sure he could not see through it at all, so I rammed my fist in front of his face like I might hit him. Over and over, I threw my hands in his face like I was fixing to smack him, and he didn't jump or flinch at all. Then I prayed for his eye to be opened.

When I finished praying, I said, "Can you see anything?"

He said, "Nothing."

I said, "Can you see my hand? Can you see those numbers on the wall? Can you see this kid?" I wanted to verify that he really couldn't see so that when God did open his eye, we would know it really was a **Miracle**.

Once again, I began to pray for his bad eye. Then I released my hand off his bad eye and covered his good eye. I said, "Do you see anything?"

He was standing there frozen. I thought, 'Oh no, is he shy too? Is he scared? Is he not going to talk to me?'

I asked him, "Do you see anything?"

Tears started rolling down his face. He said, "I see the word hallelujah up there on the wall." He began to spell it out. "I see the H-A-L-L-E-L-U-J-A-H."

Now, I had a lot of people there who were waiting to be prayed for, but this young boy received his sight, and he was looking around.

I held up my hand and I asked the young boy, "Do you see my hand? Do you see my fingers?"

I held up three fingers and asked him, "How many fingers am I holding up?"

He said, "Three."

I held up one finger and asked him, "How many?"

And he said, "One."

I held up four fingers and said, "How many fingers am I holding up now?"

He told me, "Four."

Each time I held up a different number of fingers and each time he answered me. By then he just broke down weeping. I just hugged him, and I said, "Are you scared?"

He said, "Yes. I've never seen out of this eye. Yes, I'm scared."

I asked him, "Were you born blind in that eye?"

"Yes," he told me, "I've never seen out of this eye, but I can see, I can see! I don't know what else to say."

I said, "You don't have to say anything, but thank you, Jesus." Wow! That's all we got to say.

Sometimes you don't know what to say. You're just so surprised when God shows up. Something that you have dealt with for years, something that's been a part of your life for so long that you almost give up hope that you will ever be healed. Then suddenly, God shows up and you have your **Miracle**.

You might ask yourself, "Is this for real? Am I dreaming? Pinch me!"

Glory to God it's real. When you don't know what else to say, just say, "Thank You, Jesus!"

There was so much going on that when it came time to close the meeting, no one wanted to go, and there were still people who had not been prayed for. **Miracle**s were happening everywhere, but the time for us to leave was at hand because of the contract. I said, "Maybe we can ask the janitor if he will allow us to continue."

So, they went and asked the janitor if we could stay a little longer. He was excited about the **Miracle**s too and said it was no problem because he couldn't close anyway due to the circus that was still going on next door. We were able to stay and pray for everyone that wanted prayer. More **Miracle**s happened in that auditorium than we may not know about on this side of eternity. **"It's☐a☐Miracle!"**

# MAN CAN'T LIFT HIS ARMS

I'll never forget the first time that we went to Durbin, West Virginia. We were there with Pastor David Angel who was a good friend of ours. He was an awesome pastor and evangelist. David has now gone home to be with the Lord, but we really loved him and miss him tremendously. We always loved to go see him, his wife, Sherry, and his grandson, Nathan. I would always tell everyone I have three angels, when referring to them because their last name was Angel.

I remember this service well because of all the **Miracle**s that we saw that night. After I preached at the service I said, "Now we're going to pray for people." We had the people all line up in the front of the sanctuary. Children and adults both were lined up across the front of the sanctuary. On one end there were several couples who had come up for prayer.

Randy led the way as we went to go pray for people. As we went to extend our hands towards the first ones in the line something amazing happened. Before I could even put my hands on any of them, all four couples as well as the catcher fell out. These people fell on top of the catcher and were piled up in a heap. The rest of them who wanted prayer were just looking at me and I'm like, 'I don't know what just happened.'

The pastor said to me, "Do you think they are okay?"

I said, "I don't know."

He said, "Have you ever had this happen before you came to our church?"

"No," I told him, "I haven't."

He said, "Well, let's just keep going."

Neither one of us knew what to do so we just moved on to the next person in line. This man had a bad back. We sat him in a chair to see if his back was out of alignment and we noticed that one of his legs was shorter than the other. As we prayed for him, we watched one of his legs grow out. In fact, both legs kept going back and forth. They were growing and shrinking with the other leg until both were the same length.

Suddenly that person jumped up and said, "Yeah! It feels good! No pain. All the pain is gone!"

Then we had another person whose ankles were killing him from pain. Randy and I got down on the floor and we laid our hands on his ankles. As we were praying, this person told me that they felt like there was fire in their ankles.

As God was confirming His word with signs and wonders and **Miracle**s, we just kept working our way down the prayer line praying for people.

When we saw that the pile of people on the floor were starting to stir, we went over and helped them all get up. As they were getting up, I said, "Are y'all all okay?" Because they fell on top of each other, even on top of the catcher. This catcher was buried under the four couples. We asked them what had happened, and we found out that every single one of them, including the catcher, had bad back problems and God had been healing and adjusting their backs while they were laying in that pile. I guess the Lord operated on every one of them at one time. They were all healed.

My favorite part about this night though, was when I came to one man in the prayer line.

I asked him what he needed prayer for, and he told me, "I can't lift my arms up over my head."

I said, "Well, I believe you can."

He said, "No, I cannot." And he showed us by lifting his arms only halfway up. He said to us, "This is it. This is as far as I can lift them right here."

I said to him, "Well, tonight you're going to lift your arms all the way up. Do you believe that?"

He said, "No… but yes… I don't know. But I can't lift my arms any higher."

"I said, well I believe you can." Is that what you want prayer for?"

He said, "Yes."

I said, "Do you believe you can lift your arms?"

"I don't know," he said.

I said, "Well, I do. So, let's pray." So, I prayed for him, and I said, "Now lift your arms."

He says, "I told you, I can't." He tried to lift his arms, and they only went up halfway again.

I said, "Put them back down. Let's pray again. God's going to lift your arms."

You know, sometimes you just have something within your heart by which you know, that you know, that you know. It is the Holy Spirit at work inside of you, giving you a word of wisdom, with the gift of faith and healing. I wish I could say this is always the case, but it is not. It is only as the Holy Spirit quickens it in my heart.

I do not know who all God's going to heal, or when He's going to heal, or how He is going to do it. In this situation I just knew within my heart that God was going to heal this man's arms. I was not going to stop. So, I prayed again, and I said to him once again, "Now lift your hands".

He said to me, "I told you I can't, this is it." He had lifted his arms up halfway again. Trying to force them to go higher, but they seemed frozen when he got halfway up.

I said, "Put them down. This time, we're going to pray, but before I finish praying, I want you to be thinking, I'm going to throw my arms up as high as I can. I'm going throw my arms up with all my might. And I want you to throw them up. Don't be saying I can't. I want you to throw them up. Will you do this for me?"

He said that he would try. So, I prayed again. I said, "Lord, help him. The devil has bound his arms. Devil you lose him, and you let him go right now in the name of Jesus." And then I yelled, "Throw up your arms now!!" I mean I yelled at him. Without him really thinking, he did it. At that very moment God loosed his arms.

He was so excited that he began to walk all over that church. He began to show them how God had healed his arms holding them above his head. This man was so excited about his arms being healed that he was showing everybody. Not just the people up front who were waiting to be prayed for, but also those out in the congregation.

He was telling everyone, "Look at my arms, God's healed them!"

I was told later that he even went all over that small town of Durbin, West Virginia, telling everyone what God had done for him. He went to the barbershop, and the stores, and went knocking on all the neighbor's doors all over the town.

Now they have a famous train station across the street from the church that attracts a lot of tourism. The train gives rides that are something like the Polar Express. The train would leave from this small town of Durbin and go up into the mountain and come back. People from everywhere would come into town just to ride this famous train. This man had even gone over there and was talking to all those coming in by vehicles and tour buses about how God had just healed his arms.

His story got some of these tourists curious and they began to ask him questions. He was telling them how that he was at his local church across the street and these preachers from Texas came and prayed for him. He told these people, "When my arms were healed, it scared me in the beginning. But Jesus Christ healed me, and He will heal you too."

103

Jesus is the same yesterday, today and forever. What He did over 2,000 years ago, He still does today. **"It's☐a☐Miracle!**

## CAUGHT MY MIRACLE WHILE CATCHING

Many times, in Pentecostal churches where they pray for people, they have a catcher help catching people as they fall out. People who usually serve in the ministry lines with catching, drop cloths, Kleenex handling, etc. miss out in getting prayer. I have seen God move on people serving and on the worship team who sometimes miss the opportunity of getting in the prayer line.

I was at a church up in Harrisburg, Pennsylvania, and there was a man there that was helping catch. Suddenly he and the person he was to be catching fell out. The person fell right on top of the catcher, and it knocked the catcher down. They both fell to the floor.

The catcher began to shout from the floor, "Oh my goodness, Oh my goodness. My ear just popped. I can hear, I can hear out of this ear that I could not hear from. I was deaf in this ear." He said, "God did not just heal my ear, but he also healed my back."

The catcher began to testify. "I said to myself, 'I

should not be helping catch because I have a bad back, but no one else seems to be helping.'" He got up and started running all around the church shouting and showing everybody. "Look at this, look at this! I was just going to be a catcher."

I said, "Well, it looks like you caught it."

Sometimes as a catcher you will get the overflow of God's spirit. God is so good. **"It's a Miracle!"**

## LITTLE BOY HEALED AS HE MOVED IN FAITH

Randy and I were in Petersburg, Virginia, ministering in a tent. We ended up in this tent because of a man that had approached us about it while we were in Ashland Virginia. When he met us there, he said, "I'm going to put up a tent in Petersburg, Virginia. and I want you to come speak under the tent."

I said, "All right, we would love to come. I love tent meetings. It's a part of my heritage."

I could see why God had us to go there for many reasons. Yes, it was to preach and to pray for people, but it was also to give this man some directions. We gave him some practical instructions like how he needed to get porta-potties and fans.

He also needed to spray because there were ants on the ground everywhere.

I told him, "People will not keep coming if they get bit by these ants, and there is nowhere to use the bathroom."

 This man had put this tent up in the inner-city area. The good news is that it was close to a church, so the church let this man use their electricity. God really moved on our behalf because we had this big guy that came into the meeting. He looked rough and acted like he might want trouble. It turns out this guy was the main gang leader in the area. He came in and heard the word of the Lord, and he wept, and he cried, and he gave his heart to Jesus.

During the meeting, I spoke about the **Miracle**s and healings in dad's tent and how God moved in powerful ways. After I was done speaking, people came up for prayer.

There was this one little boy there who was about ten or twelve years old. I do not know his exact age. It turns out that he had a terrible stroke at a young age. His one hand was all drawn up. And his mouth was drawn up and limp. In every meeting, he was the first one in the prayer line to get prayed for. Even if someone in the line got there before he did, he would get in front of them and come on up to be the first one to get prayer.

Every night I would pray for this boy. I would cry out and ask God to straighten out his arm and let this boy speak again. I said, "God, heal whatever is wrong that happened because of this stroke, in his brain. Whatever is wrong, heal this little boy. Lord, he has more faith than most all of us in this tent. He's the first one up here every night wanting prayer for a **Miracle** healing."

**Miracle**s were happening in this meeting. This boy was watching these **Miracle**s take place. He would even go over and sit by the person who got healed the night before. He couldn't talk so he could not ask them questions, but I'm sure the reason he sat next to them was because he had questions.

I'm sure he wanted to know how this happened for them, because it wasn't happening for him. I'm sure he had questions like, 'How were you able to get your back healed and your knees healed? How were you able to have these things happen for you?'

I knew what he was doing. It was getting close to the end of these meetings. I told everyone to come up front if they would like prayer. At the end of this service, that boy came again. He came and he passed everybody again. He came right up to the front.

I said, "You believe tonight is your night, don't you?"

107

He nodded yes as little tears were rolling down his face.

I said, "I've never seen anybody as determined and as faithful as you are. You have come to every prayer line, and you come early to church, and you've been at every meeting. I am believing that your **Miracle** is right here." And I began to pray for this boy.

When I left, this boy's hand was still drawn up, his mouth was still drooping, and he still had a limp. There was no evident change at that moment.

As we drove away in our car, I began to cry for him. I said to the Lord, "Why didn't you heal that little boy? He was in the prayer line every night. He was the biggest one on my heart. He was the one I wanted the most of all to be healed. The people we prayed for with migraine headaches, backaches, short legs, and other problems were healed. But God, he was the one that I wanted to see the **Miracle** for. I don't understand God."

Randy was trying to encourage me. He said, "Honey, healings can happen even sometimes after you leave."

I said, "I know, but I wanted to see this one. It should have happened for this little boy."

We left Virginia and went on to North Carolina. We went to a pastor's church there and we were having Thanksgiving dinner with his family. While we were eating my phone rang. I almost didn't answer the phone because it was Thanksgiving Day, and we were at someone's house, but I thought that since I didn't recognize the number, I better find out what was going on.

I answered the phone and the person on the other end said, "Is this sister Joanna Coe Herndon?"

I said, "Yes."

They said, "I called because we were not sure if you had heard about the little boy. You know the little boy that had his hand-drawn up and had a droopy mouth because of a stroke. Remember what you said to him before you left? You said to him, "I want you to go to the mirror every day. I want you to look in the mirror every day and try to speak the name of Jesus. Now, I know that you cannot speak, but I want you to try to say His name."

Now to be honest with you, I had forgotten all about the instructions I gave to him. It had been about ten days since we left the tent meeting in Petersburg. But here I was receiving a phone call about this little boy who I had wanted to be healed so bad. I remembered then that when I told him those instructions, he nodded yes with his head.

These people told me that he must have been doing it ever since I had left. They said, "We noticed it because soon his hand began to straighten up. His mouth isn't drawn up anymore and he doesn't limp anymore. The other day he walked into the room where his mother was and he said, "Jesus, Jesus, Jesus, Jesus.'"

The mom said, "What are you saying?"

He said, "Jesus!"

They told me that his mother, right then and there, had a glorious Holy Spirit fit because he was saying Jesus. His mother says he also counted to ten with his hand. **"It's a Miracle!"**

## OVERWHELMING GRIEF REMOVED

Sometimes people will call us or send us testimonies of the miraculous things that God has done for them. This is a testimony I received from Kathy Dolman concerning a healing she received at the *Women's Ingathering* meeting in Wilkes-Barre, Pennsylvania. This is her testimony:

"In June, I lost one of my best friends in this world. Becky and I met 25 years ago at a job. We were assigned a job together and within ten minutes we were instantly the closest of friends. Becky was there when I got married, watched my boys grow up and was always there when I needed a tried-and-true friend. She found out she had cancer last October and I watched her slip away in just a few short months. It tore my heart out, even though I know she went to meet the Lord.

After she died, I had this profound sense of loss. It affected me so that I was having trouble sleeping. I lost interest in many things, including my writing project. (I'm an author.) But the worst part of this depression and grief, was that I had lost the ability to intercede. Prayer and worship are like breath to me.

No matter what I did, I just would find myself unable to press in, or to lose myself in worship. I settled for worshipping Him in any way I could… pulling weeds outside the church building, vacuuming the steps in the sanctuary... I was so frustrated that I could not pray like I used to. I would begin and find my mind fogged and distracted. Worship felt perfunctory at best.

At the meeting, Joanna Coe Herndon offered to pray for intercessors that had lost their cry. I could have pole vaulted to the front of the meeting room. I have felt the Holy Spirit's touch before, but when Joanna prayed over me and tapped my head, I felt like the grief and depression escaped from me in

111

one loud burst. I have never experienced His touch like that before! I fell out in the Spirit.

When I was able to move again, I got up and began to make my way back to my seat. Halfway back, I began to laugh. The manifestation of laughter was also falling on another woman I never met before and the two of us were on our knees hugging and laughing. Not just laughing but laughing so hard we were crying.

Since that day, it feels like a dam burst. Oh, sure, I still have tearful times when I think about Becky. Part of my life is gone, but the overwhelming grief and depression is not there. I am sleeping better and waking up with enthusiasm. I've started writing again and I can enter times of intercession on a deeper level than ever before!" **"It's a Miracle!"**.

## STILL HEALED YEARS LATER

This email was sent to me from Donita Zimmerman in February 2022. I want to share it with you.

"In the year 2012 was a very rough year for me. I began having stomach issues. It concerned me because these types of issues ran in my family. In 1980 my mother was diagnosed with Chronos disease and had to have an Ileostomy and a bag was placed on her side. Later, my older sister was diagnosed with ulcerative colitis and eventually had to have an ileostomy bag as well.

When I began to have issues, I was very concerned that I might follow the same course. I saw a gastro doctor and I was told I had a little bit of both diseases. For the next few years, I had issues on and off. In 2015, I was having what the doctor called an episode, which was very painful. The meds I was taking wasn't controlling this episode very well, so of course I was praying and crying out to God for relief.

During a service at Rock of Ages Church, in which the Spirit of God was moving, my husband, Dennis, asked you to come and pray for me. I know we have a big God, and He can do all things; but at this time, I was just looking for relief of my symptoms. I was not fully expecting a healing of the issue completely. You laid your hands on my stomach in the place that it was hurting the most and began to pray. A healing began to take place in my body. It wasn't immediate for me on everything, but God over the next few weeks did heal my body.

I'm no longer on medication (praise the Lord) and the symptoms I once had to endure are no longer. Thank you, Joanna, for allowing God to use you for me. Thank you for the prayers you've prayed and continue to pray for the sick. Your gift through the

Lord is amazing and so glad you are out there spreading God's love and healing to all." **"It's a Miracle!"**

# I CAN EAT

Here's another email that was sent to me on December 27, 2021.

"This is Hannah (banana) from Jesus Is Lord in Gettysburg. I just wanted to share a little about what God has done since you guys were in Gettysburg. Long story short, the day after you guys prayed for the blood disorder, I started noticing that I was not getting headaches after I eat certain foods.

So, I decided to try more foods that would make me sick. As time has gone, I have been able to eat every food that I could not for a long time, and I feel great. Also, I have now been able to reach things on the second shelf that I could not reach in our kitchen. This has been so cool and just wanted to share." **"It's a Miracle!"**

## HEALING OF A TWISTED SHOULDER

This is an e-mail of a testimony I received from Teresa Golden in Shepherdsville, Kentucky.

"My pain started in June 2014. It was so bad that I could not even lift my arm, and when I did, I was totally twisted. My body was a mess! I was not able to dress or undress myself. The pain ran down my arm all day. I would take up to 8 Advil at a time, and this still would not relieve any pain.

I went through 8 weeks of therapy with no improvements. Therapists told the doctor there was no need to continue treatments, and that I should be referred to an orthopedic doctor. The orthopedic doctor scheduled me for surgery immediately. He said my shoulder was frozen and he was going to break it and do surgery.

I was so excited to hear you all were coming to Holy Chapel again to minister. You and Randy prayed for my shoulder. Brother Randy knew nothing about my shoulder, but while he was praying, he told me God showed him a twisted muscle. Randy said, 'I don't know if you have seen a doctor, but there is no need to have anything done to it. Just be patient because God is healing it. It may take a few days, but it will be healed.'

The next day I called and postponed my surgery

because it was feeling better. Occasionally some pain would be there as a reminder. I kept reminding God what Brother Randy said that I was to be patient and God would heal my shoulder. In faith I called back my surgeon and just cancelled the surgery. Not long after that I began to be able to lift my shoulder and the pain was gone.

God is so good. I can raise my arm as high as the other arm! This has encouraged my faith in God to trust and believe. I knew God could do it but wondered if He would do it for me. Thank You Jesus that He did it for me. I love Him so much. Thank you for being there and praying for me." **"It's a Miracle!"**

# NO MORE CHOKING

**This Facebook post was sent to us on August 25, 2013, from Diane Panunti-McDonald.**

Diane wrote, "I have an awesome testimony. For years now I have had a choking condition. After countless tests doctors could not figure out why this was happening. The Herndon's were at our church and had an altar call if anyone needed a healing in their body. My son came and sat by me and told me I needed to go up and get healed.

I hesitated at first but then I agreed. I told Evangelist

116

Joanna Herndon what was happening. Her husband, Randy said that God just showed him there is constriction and to lay hands on it and God would remove it. When he did, I felt this warm feeling in my throat. I just received a **Miracle**." **"It's a Miracle!"**

## GOD'S GLORY COMES IN WORSHIP

Kathryn Kuhlman understood the importance of worship. She was a mighty woman of God who had lots of **Miracle**s in her services, but she always had worship first to usher in the presence of God. Then she would wait for the Holy Spirit to lead and guide her.

During her worship services people would begin to be healed in their seats. Amazing **Miracle**s transpired during the worship time. People would even come out of wheelchairs. People would rise who could not even stand up, hands raised towards heaven, tears streaming down their faces as the **Miracle**-Worker was working on them and pouring out His glory over them.

I'm telling you that there is healing in singing, and there is healing in worship. Worship will bring the manifested presence and glory of God into your life as you sing of your love for Christ from your heart. Sickness, disease, and demonic powers cannot stay where the presence of God is manifested.

# CHAPTER FIVE
# SING OVER YOURSELF

I have told people to just sing over yourself because it makes the devil mad. He doesn't like you to sing over yourself. He's trying to get you down and out, discouraged, busted, disgusted and bitter. But when you begin to sing over yourself, it drives Satan crazy because his plans to discourage you won't work.

Singing is an act of faith, that even when you're feeling those things, you keep on singing and eventually these dark emotions will lift off, and you will start feeling joy and peace. I have told people to sing over your sickness, over your pain, over your problems and over your negative circumstances. God inhabits the praises of His people.

---

**"But thou art holy, O thou that inhabitest the praises of Israel" Psalms 23:3**

Here is an example of what God will do if you simply lift your voice and sing to Him. I was singing one time in a church. The song that I was singing was, "You Are Awesome in This Place, Mighty God."

I began singing, *"You are awesome in this place, mighty God. You are awesome in this place, Abba Father. You are worthy of all praise, to You our hands we raise. You are awesome in this place, mighty God..."*

On a personal note, I was just wanting us to have fun and worship, but God had other plans. God wants to set His people free because He's the Way Maker, **Miracle** Worker, and Promise Keeper. He wants you to be healed. He wants you to be delivered. He wants you to be free. He wants you to be saved.

As I was singing, I began to change the lyrics just a little bit. *"You are awesome in my body mighty God. You are awesome in my mind, mighty God. You are awesome in my heart mighty God. You are awesome in my life, mighty God."*

I was telling the people, "In whatever part of your body you are sick, declare right now; you are awesome in my kidneys mighty God. You are awesome in my knees mighty God." I was naming different parts of the body. "You are awesome in my ankles, mighty God, you are awesome in my intestines, and my digestive system." Remember, God inhabits the praises of his people!

The people were all lined across the front, waiting to be prayed for. I was going down this line of people and I was just laying hands upon them. When I got to this one lady the Holy Spirit caught my attention.

Sometimes people ask, "How do you know when to minister to somebody?"

All I can tell you is there is like a magnetic draw to them. They seem to stand out above the rest. I simply respond to that divine magnetic pull.

I just stopped and started praying for this lady. I sang to her, *"You are awesome in her mind mighty God; You are awesome in her mind, Abba Father. You are worthy of all praise, to You our lives, we raise."* I kept singing this to her, *"You are awesome in her mind, mighty God."*

Suddenly the lady began to growl, snarl, twist and turn. At that moment I realized that she needed deliverance.

How do you know when people need to be delivered? The demonic powers will manifest under the presence of God.

A demonic power was tormenting this lady's mind.

No wonder God wanted me to sing over her. There were demons who were tormenting her. I began to pray, and the more I kept singing and praying, the more the devil manifested. I was not moved by the growling, snarling, twisting, or turning. I was saying, "Shut up, devil, she's going to get free. In the name of Jesus, I break every voice, every sound, everything that you are tormenting this woman with."

At that very moment, the power of God overwhelmed her, and she ended up on the floor. Many times, I have found myself on the floor when the glory of God has overwhelmed me. I was not afraid to go to the floor with her. I went down to the floor after that devil. I kept my hands on her and kept singing, *"You are awesome in her mind mighty God, You are awesome in her mind Abba Father."*

This devil screamed something at me, but I just kept on singing. I couldn't even tell you what the devil said, and I don't care. I don't ever listen to devils, nor do I talk to them because they are nothing but liars. Satan's whole purpose is to kill, steal and destroy.

Why in the world would I entertain demonic powers that have no truth within them? There is nothing we have in common. They just need to shut up and come out! Suddenly I could see by the gift of discernment that they were coming out one after another. As the last demonic power left this woman, she became the picture of perfect freedom.

Tears began to flow from her eyes and down her precious face. Great joy overcame her as she began to experience freedom in Christ. The Holy Spirit overwhelmed her, and she began to speak in a heavenly language. She was laughing and crying and laughing and crying some more. Joy and laughter came upon all of those who were standing there. This laughter and joy became extremely contagious, and it began to hit some of the people.

At that moment I said, "Well, we're not going to do anything else. Everybody come on up here and we will just start praying for people and singing over them."

God was moving in an awesome way. God loves for us to sing and be full of joy. Heaven is full of singing. The Scriptures even say that God sings over us. He loves the worship when we do it from our heart, not our head. The Scripture declares that He is looking for those who will worship Him in Spirit and in truth.

———————————————————

*"But the hour cometh, and now is, when the true worshippers shall worship the Father in spirit and in truth: for the Father seeketh such to worship Him. God is a Spirit: and they that worship Him must worship Him in spirit and in truth"*

*John 4:23-24*

People were getting healed and set free as they were singing, and as we were singing over them.

Later, at the end of the service, we were talking to this lady. She said that ever since she was a little girl there were six different voices that began to visit her. She told me who they were. These were demonic powers that had enticed her as a little girl. They used to come to her in dreams.

Eventually, without her even realizing what she was doing, she opened her life to these demonic powers. That is when they entered her. As far back as she could remember she had fought them in her own natural ability. But that night Jesus had set her free. As I was sitting there listening to her and I was thinking, 'Wow, God, you are so awesome in how You work!' **"It's A Miracle!"**

# A BLOOD-SUCKING DEMON

I would love to tell you about a conference that I was invited to be a speaker at in Pasadena, Texas. This conference was called *Encounter with the King.* They had some well-known speakers at this conference. They may not think of themselves as well-known, but a lot of other people think so.

The speakers were Judy Jacobs, Edith and Laverne Trip, Greg and Terri Casto, and Angela Smith. Even my friends, the McDuff brothers, came to the meeting to see me. They were all wonderful speakers and great to be around. I was blessed to be to be a part of this team.

People would say, "You get to hang out with well-known people because of your dad."

We believe God opens the doors He wants open and the doors He wants shut, He will shut. I always say, if you want your name in lights, be an exit sign. The only light and the only truth are Jesus Christ. The only one we need to be looking up to is Jesus. But the sad truth is that people always exalt other people. We only have one hero, and His name is Jesus Christ.

While being surrounded by all these well-known speakers the thought came to me, 'Oh my I'm just this little person here with all these renowned people.' But they booked me, so I went.

I was thinking to myself, 'Okay, well, not very many people will come; they don't know me.' (Well, I was wrong because there was a good crowd that night. I was like, 'woah!')

It was my night to preach, and I was a little nervous because all these people had already preached. We were in their prophet's quarters at the church, and just before the meeting, some people came banging on my door.

They said to me excitedly, "Quick! Quick! Hurry! you need to get over to the office!"

And I said, "What's wrong?"

They said, "Somebody wants to talk to you."

I said, "Well, can they talk to me after church?"

They said, "No, they need to talk to you right now!"

When I got over there they said, "Edith Trip wants to talk to you."

I went into the office where she was waiting for me.

She says to me, "I want to tell you about what happened to me as a little girl at one of your dad's tent meetings."

126

Anytime I hear from people who have gone to my dad's tent revival or who were in one of my dad's church meetings, whether they were children or adults, I always want to know what happened.

I asked her, "What did you see? How was it?"

She said, "You know, I was listening to your dad on one of his radio broadcastings. He was talking about healings and **Miracle**s at his tent revival. Now, I desperately needed healing. I had gotten bit by a mosquito. The doctors did not know what disease this mosquito carried, but it infected my foot so bad that they were going to have to amputate it.

I was just eight years old at the time. When I heard your dad talking about healing in this tent revival, I said to my mom, 'Mom, before we go into surgery and do that, could we go to this tent revival to get prayed for?'

My mom said, 'Okay, I'll take you.' So, she loaded me in the car, and she brought me to your dad's tent revival.

My mom got in the prayer line with me. When we stood before your dad my mom raised me up to show him where I had been bitten by this mosquito, and my foot was all infected."

Edith Tripp continued saying, "Your dad suddenly reached down and put his hands around my ankle

127

and then he began to pray. What he said was kind of shocking to me. He said, 'You blood-sucking demon, come out of this little girl right now!'

'Wow!' I thought, 'I have a blood-sucking demon?!' But thank God your dad had cursed it and told it to go. The infection scabbed over, and the scab fell off and all I have left is this scar. I wanted to show you this scar and tell you this story about your dad, because you're Jack's daughter."

She said, "Now my grandkids run in the house with their friends and say, 'Show them your blood-sucking demon scar!' I would have had my foot amputated if it had not been for your daddy praying for me." **"It's a Miracle!"**


## COME OUT YOU BLOOD-SUCKING DEMON

I did not understand why Edith Trip told me that story about my daddy, but I have discovered through the years that many times things do not happen just by accident. God has a divine plan that he will unfold to me in time. Of course, I love to hear the stories of my father and the testimonies. Many times, I don't realize that when I hear them, God's going to use them, and I'm going to run into a situation that's very similar.

A year later, as I was getting ready for a mission trip to Colombia, South America, my husband told me that three people were going to come out of wheelchairs.

I said to him, "Like, REALLY!?"

He said, "Yes, the Lord told me to tell you THREE!"

I was like, "YES! I receive that!"

So, every church in Colombia that I went to, I prayed for those who were in wheelchairs with great expectancy. I was expecting **Miracle**s for the three! I would ask every person in a wheelchair, "Are you ready to get up and walk?"

I was at this one meeting where they had about six or seven people in wheelchairs lined up right in front of me. I'm thinking to myself, 'Wow, is this the wheelchair night? Is this the night they're going to come out?'

With the help of my interpreter, I went to the first person, and I asked him, "Why are you in this wheelchair?"

And he said, "Well, I got in a fight and got stabbed and I'm paralyzed."

And I said, "Would you like to arise and be healed?"

And he said, "Well, I'd like for you to pray for me."

I said, "I know, but are you ready to come out of that wheelchair?"

The interpreter said that the man simply wanted the pain to stop. I believe he got what he asked for, but it is a shame that people just will not look to God to be completely healed.

The second one I went to in a wheelchair, I asked, "Are you ready to get out of that wheelchair?"

I mean, I was ready to just pull them up out of that wheelchair like my daddy used to. When my daddy pulled people up out of wheelchairs, he would kick the wheelchair away from them, so they couldn't sit back down, because he wanted them to run for Jesus.

So, I was thinking, 'Let's go! Somebody's going to get out of a wheelchair. There's going to be three of you. Who's the three?'

I go to the third person. A woman was sitting there, and I said, "Why are you in this wheelchair? What's wrong with you?"

She said, "Well, I'm paralyzed from my waist down."

I said, "What happened to you? Why are you paralyzed?"

She said, "I got bit by some mosquito, some bug. I

got infected and it paralyzed me. And there is nothing the doctors can do for me. Even though the infection's no longer in there, it has left me paralyzed with this condition in the wheelchair for several years."

I said, "Really? Lean forward."

She leaned forward and I ran my hand down her back. At that moment I prayed, "You blood-sucking demon come out of her now in Jesus' name!"

I knew then what I was dealing with because of this story that Edith Trip had told me about my father. Without her telling me this story I would have never realized what was going on. I said, "In the name of Jesus, you blood-sucking demon you cannot stay in there no more."

I looked at this lady in the wheelchair and I said, "Are you ready to walk?"

She said "Yes!" Tears were rolling down her face.

I grabbed one of her arms and said, "You know, sometimes in the Holy Spirit, you feel pretty strong, and you can do stronger things than you normally could."

I told the interpreter that was standing by my side, "Get that guy and tell him to help me." This man grabbed this lady's other arm and was helping me try to pick her up out of that chair. Now remember, from her waist down she can't move. So, I'm like, "Come on and walk!"

Basically, we were dragging her because I knew she was going to walk. I just knew she was. I had faith that would not take no for an answer. So, we're dragging her. We're dragging her across the floor and speaking the name and the blood of Jesus over her. I kept saying, "You blood-sucking demon, you are gone in Jesus' name!"

Now this woman was so heavy that she was taking me to the floor, But I just knew that I knew that this woman was going to walk. At that very moment, suddenly, one of her legs came forward and went plop! And then the other leg came forward, and it went plop!

We were holding on to her as tight as we could. It was like she was completely dead weight. But when that first leg came forward, and then the second leg came forward, suddenly strength began to flood her body. She began to stand taller, but she was moving slow.

As we continued to walk at her side, she began to move a little bit faster and faster. The next thing we knew she was moving on her own. We were hardly holding her up anymore. We were just there giving her a little bit of help and support.

I said, "Let her go. Let her walk on her own." And she kept walking.

As she walked on her own, she got stronger and faster, and stronger and faster. I had more people to pray for, but I heard a noise behind me. This lady's friend was standing next to her. She was trying to tell her to get into the wheelchair so she could push her back to where they were sitting.

She told her friend, "You get in that wheelchair. I just got out of it. I'll push you!" And that's exactly what she did. I saw her put her friend in the wheelchair, and she was pushing her faster and faster. **"It's a Miracle!**

## MORE BLOOD-SUCKING DEMONS

I didn't realize that the testimonies of blood-sucking demons would continue. One time in a meeting at the Equipping Center Church in Bryan, Texas, with Pastor Jacob and Anna Biswell, God was doing wonderful **Miracle**s. Many people were getting healed. Things were happening. Word got out, and the meetings were extended.

Every night the pastor would say, "We're going to

go another night." The next night he would say, "We're going to go another night," but he would always make these announcements at the end of the service.

I thought, 'Pastor you need to announce this at the beginning of the service. You are telling them at the end of the service when most people leave a little early before the service is over. People are not going to know that the service is continuing.' Well, I was wrong, people found out and they came.

One night there we were conducting services and while I was preaching, suddenly, I perceived the Lord was nudging me. These words came to me: blood-sucking demon. I tried to ignore it because I thought it was just in my head. Then it came to me again: blood-sucking demon. I'm thinking, 'Joanna this does not fit with what you are ministering on.' I tried to ignore this thought and kept on trying to preach. But this thought was so strong in my mind that my tongue got tangled while I was trying to preach. I'm like, 'What is going on?' I finally had to stop preaching because the thought was so strong.

I switched gears and I told the congregation about my experiences with blood-sucking demons. I began to tell that first story, and then the second story from Colombia. I'm finishing up the one in Colombia and how this woman who was lame from her waist down was delivered and she got up out of her wheelchair and walked.

As I was telling this, I heard this person screaming from the back of the church. This person was screaming, "That's what's wrong with me! That's what is wrong with me! I have a blood-sucking demon!" Here popped up this lady from the back of the church where she was laying down still crying out, "I have a blood-sucking demon!"

Her friends carried her up front so I could minister to her. I found out later that had I not stopped and told that story when I did, she would have been gone. She told her friends that had brought her and laid her across the chairs in the back that she was so sick that she wanted to go home. She was so sick that before she even came, she did not want to come to the church services. But her friends told her that she needed to come because there were **Miracle**s happening every night and people were getting healed everywhere.

Her friends told her, "It's time for you to get your **Miracle** healing."

Of course, when she got the revelation of what was going on a little bit more strength entered her body. She finally realized it was a devil that was tormenting her. She came up front with tears running down her face. We began to pray over her, casting out this blood-sucking demon in the name of Jesus Christ and by His blood. We commanded her to be free in the name of Jesus. Praise God that she was healed at that very moment. That blood-sucking demon left her body and has never come back.

When we got done praying for her, she told us, "It is gone, I felt it leave my body!"

I found out later that the medical world told her that she would not live. The doctors did not know what to do with her. A mosquito carrying the dengue virus had bitten her while on a mission trip in India and poisoned her body. This disease was so bad, and her platelet count was so low that blood was coming out of her pores. The hospital, doctors and the embassy in India told her that she would not be able to go back to America with this disease. The doctors could not stop the bleeding.

She told the doctors, "I'm going home, and you cannot stop me." She told us that she knew she had to get herself out of that place.

She told me, "I got on a plane. My clothes would be soaked in blood, and I would have to change. They kept telling me that I had no hope, but I kept on saying, 'God I know that I am not going to die. I know that You are not done with me yet.' And they would look at me like something was wrong with me. And I kept saying, 'God, I know I'm not going to die. You're not through with me yet.'"

She said, "I thought when I got home somebody could help me. But nobody could help me. I tried everything I could. I researched and tried all kinds of herbs, essential oils, and natural cures but they did not work."

The doctors in the United States knew nothing about this incurable disease. Her oxygen levels kept dropping which was affecting her pancreas and liver. She would often quit breathing at night as well.

She told me, "I kept crying out to God for healing, but for some reason I could not connect."

By the time they had brought her to the meeting she was so weak that she didn't think that she could make it. She looked like she was dying.

Praise God, she kept coming back to the services after God healed her. I would have her come up and testify how the devil had attacked her with this incurable disease while she was on the mission field doing work for God. When she heard the story about the blood-sucking demon, and those hands were laid upon her in Jesus' name, she was healed. She is still alive today at the writing of this book.

I believe this is why Jesus has been having my husband and I share our stories. You see, these stories are for others to hear, that they may receive their healings and their deliverances. When I told this story, this precious sister took a hold of her

**Miracle** for herself. What God has done for one, he will do for others. As you read our stories take a hold of them and claim your healing and your **Miracle**. **"It's a Miracle!"**

# MY BACK IS ON FIRE

I was in West Virginia, holding healing services for Pastor Ryan Miller. He had moved from Fayetteville, Pennsylvania to Elgon, West Virginia to pastor Maple Grove Assembly of God.

As we finished up a service there was a lady who was present who had terrible back and shoulder problems. She was so full of pain that she was crying and moaning.

Another woman had shoulder problems for several years and couldn't lift her arm. This night everyone we prayed for (shoulders, backs, necks, and knees) were receiving healings and doing good. There was one lady whose husband was requesting prayer for his wife's healing. She reluctantly came forward for prayer. We prayed and the lady said she felt better, even though in her heart she did not believe, nor did she even want the healing.

Excitement was in the atmosphere and faith was charged because most of them who were prayed for that first night were healed. People were telling others they needed to get to the meetings if they needed healing.

The next night while I was preaching, Randy and I shared a story from another church about a lady who had terrible back and shoulder problems. She was so full of pain that she was crying and moaning. This lady was in a very pitiful condition. Even when I went to pray for her, I thought, 'Lady, if I keep listening to you, I am going to sit down and cry with you.' I mean, there's some people that can just draw you into their trauma and their drama. I thought, 'Maybe I can sing over her. I'm going to do something.' She was really bringing the atmosphere down with unbelief and self-pity.

As I was standing over the top of her, I began to run my hand up and down her back.

My husband said, "The Lord, the healer is here to heal you." He began to command her back to be healed in Jesus' name. At that very moment, supernatural, divine, Holy Spirit fire began to come into her back.

She said, "What are y'all doing to me? What are you doing?"

Randy said, "What are you talking about?"

139

She said, "What are you doing? What are you putting on me?"

Randy said, "Nothing! Here's our hands," as he held them out in front of her.

She said very forcefully, "You put something on me! I'm burning, my back is on fire!"

Randy told her, "It's not us but the Holy Spirit. He comes with fire, and He is burning up the disease in your muscles, your bones, and every part of your body."

Suddenly she yelled, "Oh! Oh!" Then she said, "This is good! I cannot remember the last time I was able to do this!" She was bending and twisting her neck, shoulders and back.

Telling these stories has a powerful impact in our services. We were exalting God and His **Miracle**-working power.

At the end of my preaching, this woman came running up to the prayer line. She was the first one in line. "That's my story!" she said.

I said, "What?"

She said, "That's me! What you described about that lady with a bad back and all, the one that God healed; that's me! That's what I need! That's what's wrong with me! My back is in so much pain!"

Now my husband had stepped out for a minute, to go to the restroom, so I was thinking, 'I need some help here,' because I knew God uses Randy a lot when praying for backs, necks, hips, and knees. I felt she needed him to pray for her. However, I did not even have a chance to tell her to wait until my husband came back. She wanted me to pray for her, right then and there.

She said, "That's what I need! Pray!"

I said, "Okay!"

I thought, 'I'll just hold down the fort, you know, till the army comes, or the troopers come, or until Randy gets back.' I just kept my hand running up and down her back speaking, "In the name of Jesus." As I was running my hand up and down her back, suddenly she started jerking like I had hooked her up to an electric shock machine. I mean, her whole body started jerking and popping and snapping. It was so violent that I took my hands off her back.

My husband could hear someone hollering all the way back to the bathroom. After a brief period of this happening, she stopped jerking. Then I put my hands back on her back and something began to happen to her back. You could hear something popping, snapping, and cracking.

I was telling her, "I'm sorry, I'm sorry, I'm not doing

this you know." I mean, one time her whole face almost went to the floor. Then another time she bent all the way backwards. I was thinking, 'What is this?' And that's about the time my husband walked up during all this commotion.

As she was going backwards and forward, she was screaming at the same time. I thought, 'how can this woman be bending and twisting like this with a bad back?'

'I bet this is really good for your back,' I thought sarcastically, because it looked painful. It looked like we took her finger and stuck it in a light socket. She was just snapping, jerking, and whipping her back all around, and her hair was flying all over the place.

My husband put his hand on her jerking body and suddenly she stopped. After she gained her composure, I said to her, "Well, how are you doing?"

She said to us, "It feels really good. Oh, this is good!" Then she began to say to her mother, "This is really great, mama. You were right, mama."

I asked, "Your mama was right about what?"

"Mama was right about me coming to church and being healed. I told her I couldn't come to church."

She said her mama told her, "You got to come! God

will heal you!" But she was in so much pain that she could not even make it for the ride to the emergency room the day before without screaming out in pain.

The lady told me, "I finally decided to come to the church services, but it hurt so bad, and I could not handle the pain. My husband drove me, and I screamed and cried the whole way here. Every time he hit a bump; I was screaming out loud. I really began to question whether I should have come.

I even told my husband to call my mother and tell her to forget it. I said this because he was hitting so many bumps coming to church. Every time he turned a corner, I thought my whole body was going to fall apart. Even when I came to the church, I was still full of tremendous pain. And during the church service I was saying, 'I can't do this all through church.' I kept thinking, 'Let's go. I can't do this.'"

But something had a hold of her, and she couldn't leave. She told me, "I wanted to leave and then I heard you tell the story of the woman's back and how she was crying and whining, and she got healed."

Now she was standing there full of joy and pain free. I mean, she just started dancing around and getting all excited. I said, "I think this girl's been healed." We even made a video of her after the church service. Yeah! What a mighty God we serve. **"It's a Miracle!"**

# A MEDICALLY VERIFIED MIRACLE

It was October 17, 2021, that Pastor Ryan Miller reached out to us through Facebook messenger to please pray for him.

He noted, "I am not making this public until at least after seeing the cardiologist. I am having an echocardiogram. It has been determined that I have aortic aneurysm of a fairly concerning size. Plans are being made to see a cardiologist ASAP, and I'm starting meds immediately to ensure that my blood pressure stays down to avoid either a tear in the aorta or the aneurysm bursting.

I had a separate aneurysm in 2015 and echo's taken before and after that God healed me. I am trusting Him to do the same again this time. Please be in prayer with me, though. The doctor had heard a murmur at my last appointment for just feeling worn down and unable to get strength back after Covid. She ordered the echo, and they found this aneurysm. Interesting, in the labs they found very low vitamin D & B - which the doctor said are double whammies for energy levels. So I am getting some answers as to why I have felt sick and not felt good for a while.

Even the aneurism discovery is good in that most people die suddenly with them, not even knowing they had it. She said 3cm is the upper end of normal. Beyond that is close checks within 6 months of each other or must do surgery. Mine is found at 4.5cm."

I know Pastor Ryan reached out to several people to help him pray. Randy and I agreed in prayer, "Doctor Jesus, take this case for a divine **Miracle** in his heart and body so Pastor Ryan will not have to have surgery. We believe the report of the Lord. His report says, 'I am healed!'. Healing is the children's bread. More **Miracle**s now in Jesus' name. Let the doctor's report say it was there, but now it's gone."

We received another message from Pastor Ryan on October 27, 2021.

"Thank you for praying for me! As follow-up, two weeks ago the echocardiogram revealed a sizable aneurysm at my heart. A CAT scan today revealed, as the radiologist said, I now have a PERFECT heart. My doctor compared reports THREE TIMES to confirm a "**Miracle**!" It was there and now it's NOT. My doctor said it was a bad report and she also has been praying for me, but now she is writing a testimony, from her perspective, as a healthcare provider, a true **Miracle**. Thanking God and grateful for your prayers and love."

Ryan Miller has written a small book about this

**Miracle** and the doctors gave documented proof. This was a medically verified **Miracle**. The name of his book is called, *"Heart of Flesh."* Ryan's heart of flesh became a new heart. God wants you to have your **Miracle** too! **"It's a Miracle!"**

## GOD RESTORES A GIRL WITH BRAIN DAMAGE

I was in Ashland, Virginia, at the Calvary Pentecostal Tabernacle. There was a girl in a wheelchair, and I noticed the mother wheel the little girl in and out of the tabernacle. I noticed them taking her up front with them to worship. We'd already been to a couple of services.

The two ladies with her would raise their hands and they would sing. Sometimes they'd even dance around her wheelchair because she couldn't get out of the wheelchair. I noticed that she could do some movements, but they were very limited. She couldn't walk. She couldn't do a lot for herself. I didn't know what was wrong with her but felt lots of compassion for her.

I wanted a chance to pray for this little girl. She was on my mind and my heart. One day I was in prayer, and I said to God, "Lord, I want to pray for that girl. God, I want to see a **Miracle**. I want to see her come out of that wheelchair. I want to see a divine **Miracle**. I do not know what is wrong with her, but I want to see her get up and walk." I was asking the Lord for this opportunity in every service. "Can I pray for her Lord? Can I pray for her?" But I didn't feel a release.

The third day they had asked me to speak in the morning meeting. After that morning's session, we told the people that we would pray for them. Now we were not the only ones praying, because they had a team of people who were designated to pray over those who need a touch from the Lord.

Now that morning after I preached, we called people up for prayer. As we were going down through the prayer line people were getting healed.

People began to grab for me because they wanted me to pray for them, But I was trying to see where this girl was; the one who was in the wheelchair that I wanted the Lord to heal so badly. I saw her and wanted to go right to her, but people were so desperate for prayer that they would not let me go. **Miracle**s were happening as we were praying for them.

As I was approaching the girl, I saw someone pray for her. Two people got her up out of her wheelchair and were laying hands on her. She ended up in the floor just lying there with her legs bent up. Now she was not the only one under the power of God, her mother was on the floor with her friend as well. The mother was on the floor and the friend was on the floor. I thought to myself, 'Well, maybe it's already happened. Maybe she already has a **Miracle**.' As I was getting ready to go past her to pray for others who were still standing and waiting, my friend, Lynn, stood in front of me. By the way that she was standing there, I perceived that she was not going to let me go by her.

I said, "What are you doing?"

She said, "You're going to pray for this little girl. I'm not going to let you go until you do."

I said, "Okay, but it looks like somebody has already prayed for her."

She said, "Yes, but she's not healed yet, and you're going to pray for her."

I had another lady assisting me in praying for people. Her name was Helen. She was working alongside of me as we were praying for people.

When we came to where this girl was on the floor, her knees were in the air because her legs were not straight. They were in a strange position where they were locked in to stay that way. Whether she was in the wheelchair or on the floor, they were bent in a strange, weird way.

I said to Helen, and those around us, "What happened to this little girl?"

They said, "Well, all we know is that she went through brain surgery, they took out part of her brain. This caused her muscles to begin to draw up. This affected her legs, her arms, and her hands."

I went to the top of her head and begin to pray for God to restore her brain, brain cells, and whatever had been destroyed and taken out. I said, "God, I'm asking you to begin to restore what the doctors have taken out. I'm asking you to do a creative **Miracle** and put the brain cells back.

I'm asking you to heal this little girl in the name of Jesus Christ. I want her to be healed and made whole. I don't know what all is going on. Lord, I have been asking you for the last few services. I want to see a **Miracle**. I know that you still do **Miracle**s today."

Now what I am about to tell you had to be God. I did not even think about what I was about to do. If this had not been the Lord, her bones would have snapped like brittle branches.

I said, "Okay, Helen, I want you to get on the other leg and me on this leg. Don't get ahead of me and I won't get ahead of you. And at the same time in unison, I want us to slowly bring these legs down as we say, 'In the name of Jesus.' I want these legs to straighten out. That way we will be able to lift her up because I believe she's going to walk and she's going to need her two straight legs."

As we were looking at each other and saying, "In the name of Jesus," we began to slowly push down on her knees in the air. Helen had one knee and I had the other knee. We did not get ahead of each other as we eased her knees to the ground.

When the brain is damaged, they said it literally causes your legs, hands, and arms to lock in place. She was twisted up and locked into position. So for us to be forcing those legs could have injured her. I didn't know until later that we could have broken her legs, I just perceived that this was what we were supposed to do. We were working these legs in the name of Jesus.

Suddenly I said, "Now stand her up." Her hands were still locked shut.

I said to this girl, "Are you ready to walk?"

She responded the best that she could.

I said, "I guess that means yes." I was talking to her as I was trying to help her walk. In a very short time, you could feel the stiffness of her locked arms start to loosen up. She was beginning to walk, and we could see some movement in her hands.

As we were working her muscles and her body, I was thanking God. I was saying to the Lord, "God, I know you are restoring the brain cells. Thank you, Lord. I love you, Jesus. This is awesome." Of course, there was a whole bunch more people for me to pray for. I thought, 'I can't walk her all day,' even though I wanted to.

We could tell that she did not want to stop walking. She had not been out of that chair in years. Now she was walking and did not want to stop. So, I turned Jim Edwards, who was helping me walk her; then to another one of the other men there who was helping catch and I said, "Get on this side and take my place. When she gets tired, sit her down. We're believing God for her to be completely restored."

I went on praying for more people. I was over there praying, and I heard this screaming and hollering. I'm like, 'What's going on? What?' You know, when Holy Ghost people start screaming and hollering you know something is going on, and you are missing the action.

During that time, Jim came running over to where I was at. He said to me, "She's running and she's running all by herself. She's doing it without any help. She's running on her own!!"

As I begin to turn around, she ran right past me. Her mother, who was laying on the floor under the power of God, began to stir, and she saw her girl running.

The mother said, "Jesus!"

The girl stopped in front of her and said, "Is Lord," in a very broken twisted sound. These were her first words in a long time.

Later, I discovered she was not a little girl. She was thirty-six years old. I have been told that when your brain doesn't develop, neither does your body. She had many birthdays, but her body did not develop. So what looked like a 12-year-old little girl, I found out was a 36-year-old woman. The parents told us that when the doctors went in to do surgery, they had made a major mistake.

The brain began to bleed, and they could not stop the bleeding. The operation that was to help her, did the absolute opposite. They ended up taking out a lot more of the brain because of the brain bleed. They were just going in to do what they thought was a small surgery, that became a major surgery and basically destroyed her life. But now here she was. This was just the beginning of her **Miracle**.

After the service this young lady began communicating with her mom as the people took her out to put her in the car they rented. They didn't think she knew where they were and what they rented, but she was able to recognize the rental car. They were always careful to make sure she was familiar with all her surroundings.

When they were leaving the hotel to come back to the services, she walked right up to the door of the motel room where they were staying, which was not normal. The part of the brain that they had to remove, was the part that gave her recognition, but now here she was recognizing her surroundings like she never did before.

The next night at praise and worship, this young lady's mother and friend were not able to enter into worship, because the girl was all over the place. She could not sit still because of her freedom and her healing. She was trying to speak, but her vocabulary was still a little bit confusing.

I said to the mother, "God started it, now you get her into speech therapy and physical therapy for her to develop more and get stronger."

The next year somebody sent me a video of people worshiping at Calvary Pentecostal Tabernacle. And there was this girl right up front with her mother and her friend, worshiping God with her hands lifted towards heaven.

When I saw the video, I began to exclaim, "That's her! That's her! Look what the Lord has done!"

I see people that the devil is viciously attacking, because he is out to kill, steal and destroy. I say,

"God, that's not abundant life. That wheelchair is not abundant life. That backache, headache, and affliction are not abundant life. And God, You said that You came to give life, and life more abundantly." **"It's a Miracle!**

# CHAPTER SIX
## GOD SUPERNATURALLY HEALS SCOLIOSIS

My husband, Randy, and I do not like to see people suffer. When we pastored, we would stop preaching if we noticed that somebody was suffering in the church. We would tell the people that we did not want them to suffer and that we would pray for them right then.

Sometimes we would see someone coming through the door with pain, and immediately we would go and pray for that person. Many times, we have seen **Miracle**s even before the preaching or the singing starts.

As you look at the ministry of Jesus, He was constantly setting the people free by the power of the Holy Spirit. He's a **Miracle** worker.

You do not have to set up an elaborate atmosphere to see **Miracle**s happen. Even though it's nice to be in a good atmosphere, this does not have to exist for God to heal. When the compassion of God comes upon us, and we simply respond, that is the atmosphere for **Miracle**s. The Scriptures declare that Jesus moved with compassion, and He healed them.

*"And Jesus went forth, and saw a great multitude, and was moved with compassion toward them, and he healed their sick."* **Matthew 14:14**

Once I was in Litchfield, Illinois holding meetings. In one of the services, I noticed right away that there was a lady sitting on the front row. She had to use a walker to help her walk. This lady was full of pain. I could hear her during worship service as she was crying out.

When the worship service was over, I thought, 'Well, Lord, I don't want her suffering and making these noises the whole time I'm preaching,' So I decided to do something about it. I just went over to her, and I said, "Honey, are you okay? What's wrong with you?"

She said, "I have scoliosis. I'm in a lot of pain all the time."

This disease had ravaged her to where her body had shrunk down to about four feet tall. Her body was all crooked and her bones were all messed up.

I said, "I don't know what scoliosis is. Is it something

to do with the back?"

She said, "Yes."

I said, "All right, lean forward."

I just began to pray and commanded these bones to come into alignment. I prayed, "Whatever's going on, in the name of Jesus you foul devil of scoliosis, whatever you are doing, get out, and quit tormenting this lady. Quit doing this to her"

As I was praying, she began to scream, "Oh! Oh! Oh! Oh!"

I thought, 'What is going on now?' I thought I was going to calm her down, but she got louder. She got worse.

I said, "What's happening? How are you?"

She just kept hollering, "Oh, oh, oh, oh!"

I thought, 'Well, I don't think I can preach with this going on.' So, I just simply stood over her and prayed. Finally, she got quiet for a minute.

I'm like, 'Wow!' Everybody was looking at me. I didn't know what else to do so I prayed for her again.

She kept screaming at times while I was preaching. I would go over and pray for her through this whole event, then I would go back to preaching. By the time I had finished my sermon, God had done a **Miracle** in that woman's back.

Her body was snapping, cracking, and popping the whole time. By the time God was done adjusting her back she had grown from four feet to almost five feet tall. I believe that God was snapping all her bones and vertebrates and disks into their proper place supernaturally and that was what was making her holler.

I thought, 'I didn't mean to hurt you.' But I think God wanted everyone there to know that He was working on her during the service. He was putting everything in order.

At the end of the sermon, I said, "I'm going to pray for the sick."

This lady spoke up and said, "Look!"

She stood up and held her walker in the air. She said, "Look at this. All of you know that I came in as a cripple."

When she stood up, the place went wild with people screaming, hollering, clapping, and cheering. She said, "When I came in here, I could barely get to my seat, and now I am healed."

There were three people in the prayer line that night that I prayed for who had scoliosis. One of them stated that it was just beginning to happen in their body. They said, "The doctors have examined me and ran tests, and the diagnosis is that it is scoliosis."

Another person said, "I've been having some

problems with my back, and they told me that it was scoliosis."

As I prayed for these people, their backs began to snap, crackle, and pop. They said they felt heat in their back and the pain they felt was gone. God healed all three of them of scoliosis that night. These people went back to their doctors, and the doctors could not understand how their spines straightened up. I told the pastor to tell them that they went to see another doctor. His name is Doctor Jesus. **"It's a Miracle!"**

# SUPERNATURAL WEIGHT LOSS

I was in a service in a church in Oklahoma City, Oklahoma, when I came across a lady who had a weight problem. Now, this lady was not huge, but she was overweight. It wasn't caused because she couldn't control her appetite. There was something blocking her from getting rid of this weight. She had done everything she could possibly think of to lose weight and yet she could not lose it.

I cried out to God on her behalf, and I said, "Lord, I'm asking you right now, in the name of Jesus, just to begin to let her have supernatural weight loss. Do a **Miracle** for her in Jesus' name and heal this body."

After the service she noticed her pants were loose

on her. She lived across the street from the church, so she ran next door and pinned her pants. She was telling the pastor about how she had just lost inches in her waist and had to go pin her pants.

Well, they had a dinner at the church after the teaching and ministry. This lady suddenly announced that she had to go.

She told the pastor, "I'll be right back."

The pastor said, "What?"

She said once again, "I got to go home to my house, but I will be right back."

We found out later that she was having to hold her pants up because they were loose, and she was afraid they were going to fall down. She was experiencing supernatural weight loss right then and there.

She told us later that right after prayer she began to lose weight. She had gone into the bathroom and pinned her pants up. The weight began to come off so fast though, that the pins were no longer working.

She ran home and found some smaller pants and put them on. Then she came back to eat with all of us. While we were eating, she said, "I must go again, my pants are too big."

Now she had put on a smaller pair of pants when she went to her home. She was telling us that they had been tight around her waist when she put them on, but these new pants which she had just put on were now loose. She was desperately trying to hold these pants up.

She asked me, "How much longer is this going to go on?"

I said, "I don't know, but I need some of that."

Whatever was wrong with her body, God had healed it. But not only did He heal her body, He began to take the weight off that was caused by this infirmity. God is the healer. He wants to heal and set people free. Who the Son sets free, is free indeed. **"It's a Miracle!"**

## TENT REVIVAL IN DUNN, N.C.

Now we were in Dunn, North Carolina. A lot of things happened there in this tent revival. One day a car pulled up outside of the tent. The worship had just started for the service. I saw about three or four people over by this car trying to help somebody out of it. It must have taken them ten minutes or more to get them out of the vehicle. I thought, 'What in the world, what's happening over there?

Finally, they were able to get this person out of the car into a wheelchair. She must have been way over 400 pounds. I found out later that she had to have a very special wheelchair made for her because of her size and weight. It also turned out that she could not even turn herself over in her bed or get out of bed by herself because she was so big. She couldn't do anything for herself. They wheeled her into the tent and brought her up to the front row.

I got up to preach and there was this lady sitting in this wheelchair. I'm thinking, 'She can't breathe.' I could hear her wheezing as she was trying to breathe. I'm like, 'Oh, Lord.' I thought she was going to die right there in front of us. Remember it took everything for this woman to get out of that car.

She couldn't catch her breath. I'm thinking, 'God, is she going to die?' I'm like, 'Lady, you better not die, you're not dying in this meeting, I'm trying to preach.'

Finally, I had to stop, and I told the people who were there, "Excuse me, for just one moment." I walked right down to this lady, and I said, "Hey, are you okay?"

She's trying to tell me she can't breathe.

I said, "That's okay. In the name of Jesus, I command breath into these lungs."

And I just began to pray, "Lord, I don't know what's going on. I don't even know why she got this big. I don't even know why she has this problem, but I'm also asking You, Jesus, to give her supernatural weight loss. Let this woman begin to lose weight.

Immediately get all this fat off her so she can breathe better and heal these lungs and heal whatever's going on." I was just laying hands on her and praying.

I said, "Now breathe, breathe in the name of Jesus." And she began to breathe, and I'm like, "Hallelujah, praise God!" I went back up and just preached up a storm and had a good time. At the end of the service, she called the pastor over. She was over there excitedly showing the pastor something about her pants. She was pulling her waistband away from her body.

She said, "I think I've lost eighty or a hundred pounds."

He's like, "Well, TMI." He said he could see all the way down her leg.

The next morning was Sunday, so the service was moved from the tent to the church building. This lady drove herself to the church. She got out of her car by herself, and she walked into the church and up to the front row. You must remember this woman couldn't even turn in her bed, much less, get out of a car. She said, "I want to do as much as I can for myself now that I am able. Those of us who were there could hardly believe this was the same lady.

She told us with great excitement, "I have lost 180 pounds. I can turn over in my bed. I can get up and cook. Not only that, but I have put me and my little boy on a diet. But I'm losing weight without the diet."

God was just supernaturally dropping pounds off of her.

Her little boy was also getting healthy by eating right. He was a heavyset little boy, but God was working. She boldly declared, "I'm no longer going to take the shortcut. I'm parking at the end of a parking lot, and I'm walking as far as I can walk. You see, I never could walk before much less turn in my bed, and look what God is doing."

The Pastor said, "Well, we do need to buy you some new pants before they fall off and you embarrass us all." **"It's a Miracle!"**

# GOD HEALING DAMAGED EYES

I loved being in Dunn, North Carolina in the tent meetings that my pastor friends were having. It reminded me of the old-time tent revivals with my father. It was an amazing and wonderful time praying for sick people and watching them get healed. People were coming out of their wheelchairs and were getting rid of their crutches.

But I'll never forget this one night. My husband decided to pair up with Pastor Allen Mason, who was sponsoring the tent meeting. Pastor Allen really wanted his wife, Pastor Reba, to have an opportunity to pray for people too. She was always playing the keyboard and leading worship.

I said, "All right, see if someone else can do the music. I would love to have your wife at my side ministering with me."

Randy and Pastor Allen went one way, and Pastor Reba and I went the other way. We had both started at opposite ends of the line and worked our way to the middle.

As the four of us started to meet in the middle of the line, I heard my husband say to this lady, "Do you believe God can heal you?"

She said, "No."

He said, "Well, what'd you come up here for?"

She said, "I don't know."

Randy said, "If you don't believe God can heal you, then I don't know why we would be praying for you." Then Randy and Pastor Allen just walked away from this lady.

When I heard this, I said, "Oh no, no, no, no, no, no. Wait y'all!" I didn't even think, I just walked off and left Pastor Reba praying for somebody. I told them, "I heard that. She had to believe something, she walked up here did she not?"

I turned to the lady and said, "Ma'am, you walked up here. You had to believe something, surely, or you would not have come up here."

She said, "I really do not know why I came up here."

I said, "I do. I believe you wanted prayer." I asked her, "What do you need prayer for?"

She told me that she had terrible scratches on her eyes. It was like somebody took their fingernails and scratched her eyeballs. She told us that when she looked through her eyes, she saw several of me. She said, "It's like 16 scratch marks." They were so bad that it made her almost blind.

I told the guys, "We've got to pray for her."

They responded, "Well, she says that she does not believe."

I said, "I know, but she came to the tent meeting, and she came up here into the prayer line. She had to believe something to be here. Even if she does not believe, I am going to believe with her and for her."

I told Randy and Pastor Allen to come back. I said to them, "I believe! I believe God's going to heal her!"

And they're like, "FINE!" So, they reluctantly walked back over.

I got my hands on this lady's eyes and started praying. Now, she was still a little upset because of what my husband and Pastor Allen had said to her and that they walked away from her, so I tried to calm her down by rubbing my hand along her back and talking to her real sweet.

I said, "It's okay honey. It's okay. We're going to pray for you. It's okay. Thank you for coming up. We're glad you came. We're glad you are here."

She kind of made a face at them as they were trying to say something to her. She wouldn't look at them. I mean this lady was so upset. She was just looking at me. About that time, Pastor Allen said, "Look at me! Look at me now!"

Pastor Allen was a very tall man; about six feet and eight inches tall. He had to kind of squat down to look into her eyes because she was a little short lady who was only about five feet tall.

Pastor Allen told this lady, "Look at me, Look at me now!" But she just backed up away from him.

I told her, "It's okay, look at him"

He said, "God's healing your eyes right now. Do you hear me? Look! Look! Look now!" It was a divine authority that began to rise in him.

At the same time the compassion of God was overwhelming me for her. I said to her, "Yes, God is healing you right now."

Randy said, "All right, in the name of Jesus, be healed."

We all began speaking and praying over her, and as we were, she blurted out, "I can see! I can see you! I can see! I can see you!"

She grabbed me and hugged me and cried on my shoulder. I turned to Pastor Allen laughingly and said, "If you would have been a little nicer, she would have hugged you."

She was so excited. All the scratches were gone. God had given her perfectly clear vision.

At that moment my husband spoke up and declared, "God is healing people's eyes right now. Come on to the prayer line. Those of you who have problems with your eyes, get up here!" He began to pray for people with eye problems. My husband was just praying for eyes and some of them were telling us that they could see better and were taking their glasses off.

There was this one lady who said, "I don't know. I just don't know."

I told her, "It's okay. We believe God's doing it for you."

Well, we get a call the next day from Pastor Allen. He told us that she was screaming on the phone. "Go tell them I can see! Tell them it's for real! Go tell them!"

Pastor Allen said, "What are you talking about?"

She was so excited that Pastor Allen couldn't even understand what she was saying. He told her, "Slow down so I can understand what you're saying."

She said, "Well, today I got up. I went in my office

because I needed to get some bills paid and get things done before the meeting tonight. I was working away when suddenly I realized I didn't have on my glasses. I can see everything! Before they prayed, I couldn't see anything without my glasses. Jesus has healed my eyes. Oh, hallelujah!" **"It's a Miracle!"**

## MASSIVE HEALINGS OF EYES IN JACK COE'S MEETINGS

My dad used to ask people when they got in his prayer line, "Do you want God to heal your eyes?"

"Of course," they would tell him, "Yes."

My dad would tell them, "Give me your glasses." They'd take them off and hand them to him. My dad would throw them on the ground and stomp all over them. He would tell the people, "You're not going to need this no more."

You could see the people in panic because he was over 300 pounds, and their glasses were now smashed and shattered on the ground with their frames all cracked and bent.

After he did this, He said, "Now, are you ready to

believe?"

Of course, they responded with, "Yes, I got to believe now, you just smashed my glasses, and I can't afford new ones."

One night there was a man standing in my dad's prayer line who needed his eyes healed. He saw my dad do this before and so he said to my dad as he was tightly holding on to his glasses, "You're not going to break my glasses are you? I'm not going to give them to you if you are going to stomp on them."

My dad promised him that he wouldn't stomp on them.

The man said, "Are you sure? I'm going to give them to you if you promise not to stomp on them."

Jack said, "I promise you. I'm not going to stomp on your glasses." So, the man handed his glasses to my dad.

My dad said to this man, "Now close your eyes. I'm going to pray." But what my dad did not tell him is that he had a little device in his pocket. And so, he is holding on to these glasses, and while he's having everybody pray, and believe with him, he is poking out the lenses with this little device.

My dad had an assistant there who had put his hands over the man's eyes. While my dad was poking the lenses out of this man's glasses, he asked the man, "Do you believe that God is going to heal your eyes?"

The man said, "I guess I do."

My dad said, "Well, I believe God has healed you." He then had the assistant remove his hands from the man's eyes. He handed the man back his glasses and told him to put them on.

Then my dad said, "Bring me a Bible." They rushed a Bible over to him.

He said to the man, "Read this, go ahead read this." He shoved the Bible underneath this man's face. So, the man starts reading it.

He said, "But Brother Coe..."

My dad interrupted him and said, "Read more! Go ahead read some more!"

He said, "But Brother Coe, I'm trying to tell you. I can read with my glasses on."

My dad said, "Really!"

My dad then took the glasses off the man and showed him that the lenses had been removed from his glasses. God had healed his eyes without him even knowing it. **"It's a Miracle!"**

# LOOKING FOR A MIGHTY AWAKENING

God wants to heal your eyes, your nose, your throat, your back, your fingers. I mean, He cares so much about you. Just like a little child comes running into a mama saying, "Mama I cut my finger. I got a boo-boo."

And what is a mama doing? Mama gently kisses the boo-boo and tells her child, "It's going to be okay."

Jesus cares that much about you. He's got every hair numbered on your head and when you're hurting and when you're in pain and when your tormented and you're in sickness, He cares about you.

That's why Jesus went to the man at the pool of Bethesda. The man had lost all hope because he had been in this condition for thirty-eight long years. All he could do was look to man. He said, *"I have no man to put me in the water."* (See John 5).

People are looking to man today when Jesus is right there. People are looking to the arm of the flesh to help them when they really need to look to Jesus

I asked God, "Why are we not seeing the **Miracles** like in my dad's day?" I know me and my husband are seeing them, but in many of the churches where we go, they are not experiencing these, **Miracles**. I mean, in the early church people were coming to the gathering of God's people for their **Miracles**. In my dad's day, thousands of people came nightly to the meetings to get healed. They came out of wheelchairs, off the crutches, off the hospital stretchers.

They came not just because it was a tent revival. Even when the tent picked up and left town, people would go into the churches that believed in **Miracle**s and healing. There were lots of Pentecostal churches who believed in faith, and in healing, **Miracle**s, signs, and wonders, and the people would testify about how God had healed them and delivered them. We need a mighty outpouring of the Holy Spirit. We need to get back to the power and **Miracle**s of the early church.

I travel a lot and see lots of billboards. I have noticed how so many of them are advertising for hospitals, doctors, and nurses. They tell you that prescriptions can be your answer, and your total help. They have pictures of these loving, kind faces who are ready and willing to take care of you. The billboards are stating, "Come on over to our place, come to this doctor, or that doctor. We can take care of your problems."

I'm not opposed to doctors, nurses, hospitals, or medicine. They have helped many and will continue to help many more. But it's when people look to man more than God, then I have a problem.

Jesus was standing right next to the man at the pool of Bethesda and asking him, *"Wilt thou be made whole?"*

And the man said, "I have no man..."

Jesus, the Healer, and the Great Physician, was standing right next to him, and he was still looking to man.

I told God, "I'm ready for a mighty outpouring of Your Spirit."

People need to get their eyes back on Jesus and begin to call out and cry out to Him. We need to get so determined, and we need to have so much faith, that we will push through the circumstances, push through the situation, and push past the pain to get to Jesus. Doctor Jesus wants to heal you.

# HOSPITAL ESCAPE

My dad owned a radio station in Waxahachie, Texas, and he would broadcast on the air at local radio stations in every city and state he traveled. They didn't have TV back then, but everyone would listen to the radio.

One day there was a man in the hospital listening to one of my dad's radio broadcasts. He was talking about the wonderful **Miracle**s that were happening in the tent revival. This man who was sick in the hospital was so excited that he called his wife to come to the hospital. When she got to the hospital, he told her, "Honey, tomorrow night when you come to visit me, bring my clothes."

She asked him, "Why? For what?"

He told her, "We're going to sneak out of here. I want to go to that tent meeting. I've been listening to it all day on the radio. God is doing **Miracle**s in this tent meeting. Blind eyes are being opened, the lame are walking, and people with all kinds of incurable diseases and sickness are being healed. We've got to go there. I know I can be healed."

She said, "Honey, we cannot sneak out of the hospital. The doctor told you that you cannot have any movement or stress. Remember you have all these tumors in your stomach, and if any one of them ruptures, it could lead to death. Not only that, but you have a bad heart. I do not want you to have a heart attack. Remember you are not supposed to get upset. You are not supposed to move around. That's why they have that special girdle on you to hold everything in place."

He said, "Do not worry about none of that, were going to get out of here. We're not going to tell the hospital personnel or the doctor. Then after the tent meeting, we will sneak back."

She said, "No, honey, I am not doing that." She kept on trying to talk sense into him.

This man said, "No, bring my clothes to me!"

She kept trying to tell him to calm down and quit

175

talking such crazy nonsense. She said, "You're not supposed to get upset like you are right now."

She went out and got the nurse and told her, "Something's wrong with my husband. He is talking crazy. What have they done to him here?"

The nurse tried to comfort this woman and assured her they had not done anything to her husband.

The wife said, "Well, he keeps talking crazy, about going to some tent meeting."

The nurse said, "Oh honey, when they're in the hospital a long time like this, they get a little crazy. You go home and go to bed. We'll take care of him."

So she went home and the next night she went back to the hospital after work. Her husband motioned to her to shut the door.

"Did you get my clothes?" He asked her. She didn't answer him. So once again he said, "Did you get my clothes?"

"No, I didn't get your clothes," she replied.

He said, "Why didn't you get my clothes? I told you to bring my clothes so we can sneak out of here tonight."

"Because we're not going anywhere. You are still talking crazy. I thought you would have been better tonight," she said.

"Yes, we are," he said, we're going to that tent

meeting. We are going to sneak out of here when they turn down the lights. (Back then they turned the lights out at eight o'clock.) I told you about this last night."

She said, "I told you that you are not going. We can't do that. Remember you have heart problems and tumors that could rupture. You have to be very careful."

He said, "Yes, we can go! Give me my clothes!"

She said, "I didn't bring them. And you're not going to do anything. You're talking even crazier than you have ever talked."

She went and got the nurse again. The nurse told her to go home. "It'll be okay when he gets some sleep tonight. Probably tomorrow, he'll be a little better." She left and went on home.

At eight o'clock that night when the lights went down, the man grabbed a sheet and wrapped it around himself. Then he climbed down the fire escape. He went over to a taxicab driver who was sitting at the hospital waiting for a customer. He picked up a stick along the way and when he got to the taxicab driver, he shoved that stick into that sheet and told him to take him to such and such an address.

When that taxicab driver saw that sheet bulging out from the stick, he thought it was a gun, so he didn't argue with the man, he just took him over to my dad's tent meeting.

When they got there the man told the driver, "Wait right here. I'll be right back."

They asked the taxicab driver later why in the world did he stay? He said, "I guess I was scared that the man had that gun, and I wasn't sure what he would do."

The sick man ran over to one of the ushers in the tent. He said to the usher, Give me $1.25! Hurry!"

So, he got the $1.25 and went back and paid the cabdriver and told him, "Thank you."

When it came time for prayer, my dad saw this man coming in the prayer line with this sheet wrapped around himself. Now, all kinds of crazy people would show up to my dad's meetings. Some would say they were Elisha, or Moses, or a prophet sent by God. My dad was kind of used to these kinds of things happening, so this night, when he looked down from the stage, he thought, 'Oh, who's this coming tonight? Moses? Elisha? Because here's this guy wrapped in this sheet and he's getting closer and closer.'

Finally, this man got up to my dad and my dad said, "Sir, what's wrong with you? Why are you here?"

He said, "I have these tumors and a bad heart. I'm not supposed to be moving about. I climbed down a fire escape. I've escaped from the hospital. And I want to be healed. I have been listening to your radio broadcast. My **Miracle** is here tonight."

My dad said, "Yes, it is!" and he laid hands on that man.

The minute he laid hands upon that man, that man took off running. My dad said he did not know if the man turned into Superman or what, because the sheet was flying behind that man as he was running.

My dad said to some of the men who were working with him, "When he slows down, take him into the back into the prayer tent. I want him to check and see where those tumors went."

When the man went back to check, he discovered all the tumors were gone. The man removed his girdle and came out waving that girdle and running again. He was declaring what God had done. He said, "All the tumors are gone, and my heart feels great!" This man had enough faith to escape from the hospital to get to the meeting. His heart was healed that night and all the tumors were gone.

Sometimes you must push through the circumstances. Sometimes you need to be like that woman in the Bible with the issue of blood and push your way through the crowd to get to Jesus and grab hold of the hem of His garment. **"It's a Miracle!"**

# A FOUL DEMON OF CANCER

My father prayed for a man who had cancer. on one whole side of his face. My dad spoke to the demonic power, "You foul demon of cancer come off this man now!" Then he reached out his hand to this man's face and grabbed that ugly, terrible growth of cancer. He literally grabbed, pulled, and twisted it right off the man's face.

Thousands of people were in the tent that night, and they saw him do this. He held the cancer in his hand and said, "Tell me this is not a demon."

The tentacles on the end of the cancer were wiggling. He threw this cancer on the ground, and the cancer began to move around.

My dad told them, "Do not be afraid, I have bound that demon of cancer, and he cannot touch you."

Then my dad said, "You foul demon of cancer, I curse you back to the pits of hell where you came from!" In front of everybody's eyes the cancer shriveled up and disappeared. **"It's a Miracle!"**.

# CHAPTER SEVEN
## GOD REVEALED AND HEALED

I was at a prayer meeting one night in the Chambersburg, Pennsylvania area. One of the ladies who was at the prayer meeting waved me over. She told me that she had a tremendous testimony, and she was looking for my husband, Randy. When the prayer group found out he was not there they were kind of disappointed. She had already shared her testimony with them before I came.

She said, "You know when you and your husband were at Pastor David and Carol's church in Fort Loudon, Pennsylvania, your husband came over to me and he said, 'I know you've been worried and afraid.'"

She then told me the story. She said, "There was a lot of pressure on my chest. I was having a lot of health issues and hadn't told anyone. I'm a schoolteacher so I just kept praying and asking the

Lord to just help me get through the school year and to please not let anything happen to me.

I thought it was my heart and I was having trouble breathing at night and horrible congestion. Your husband came over to me and he said, 'I want you to know it's not your heart. You've been in a lot of pain, and you're scared. You think it is your heart. If you have been to the doctors, and they have told you that it was your heart, I want to tell you, it's not your heart.'

I told him, 'No, I have not been to any doctor.'

He said, 'Well, I see it.'"

There are times when the Holy Spirit will allow Randy to see inside of people's bodies and will show him things.

"Randy said to me, 'I see it and it is an infection in your lungs.' He then described where the infection was located. He said, 'I believe right now, as I lay my hands on you, that infection is going to go away, and you're going to be healed.'

Your husband laid his hands on me, and immediately I felt good. No more symptoms, no more pain, no more congestion. That was over three years ago. That infection left and it has never come back. Tell your husband thank you for obeying the Lord." **"It's a Miracle!"**

# MOVE YOUR CAR

You know, sometimes even when people don't have faith and believe, God still does it. I would rather you believe. And I would rather let faith ignite because faith takes a hold of God, and God does the **Miracle**s. Faith requires action, because without works, faith is dead. But I have seen God heal some people even when they did not have any faith.

---

*"For as the body without the spirit is dead, so faith without works is dead also."* **James 2:26**

---

I love the story of the man who came into my dad's tent meeting. This man walked up and said to some of my dad's workers at his tent revival, "Whose car is this parked right there? Whoever it is I need them to move this car right now."

They finally got ahold of my dad. He came over and he said, "Yes, can I help you?"

The man said, "Yes, sir, is this your car?"

And my dad said, "Yes."

He said, "Sir, could you please move your car?"

My dad replied, "Well, can I ask you why you want me to move my car?"

He said, "Yeah. I need to get my wife out of our car, and she is disabled. She's paralyzed from her waist down. I need to pick her up to carry her into the tent. This car is parked right where I need to go in. It's a better location to get her in the tent. Then after this service is over with, I can pick her up and carry her back to the car. It makes it way easier for me if you can have that car moved."

My dad said, "Well, why don't I just get in your car and pray for her to be healed? It will make it easier for both of us."

He said, "No, sir, please just move your car. I have been taking her to a lot of healing meetings. This is how it works. She wants to go, so I bring her. So, here we are. Please just move your car.

So my dad moved the car. People later asked him, "Brother Coe, why didn't you just go ahead and pray for her?"

My dad said, "Because the man said no, so I moved my car."

In the prayer line came this man with his wife. He did not realize that it was my dad who was doing the meeting. When he saw my dad, he said, "I'm sorry I asked you to move the car. I didn't know it was you doing this meeting."

My dad said, "It's alright," and he began to pray for this woman; commanding her to be healed in the name of Jesus.

When he finished praying, she proclaimed with great excitement, "Brother Coe, I'm healed! Brother Coe, I'm healed! I'm healed!"

My dad responded, "Yes, sister, I believe you are."

The husband who was standing there watching all of this said, "That's what she always says in every healing meeting."

As the man was carrying his wife away from the platform she was still shouting, "I believe I am healed!"

At the end of the service, when he was taking her out of her wheelchair to get ready to go get in the car, she hollered again, "Brother Coe, can you hear me? I really believe this time I am healed."

My dad heard her shout from her car, and he responded, "I believe you are healed too."

And her husband said, "Honey, you can't even walk." So, he lifted her out of the wheelchair and put her in the car. He took her home and put her in the bed.

Now the next morning their children came over to their house to check on her. They would always come over to check on their mom after she had attended a healing meeting. When they came in the house they asked their dad, "Well, dad, what happened? How's mom?"

He responded, "The same. It is always the same as

before. You know, she's in bed. I put her in bed, and she is resting."

They were all very disappointed. Now the mother who had awakened, was in her bed listening to her children talking in the other room. She prayed, "Oh Lord, I 'd love to be in there with my kids and fix them breakfast like I used to."

As she was speaking to the Lord, suddenly she heard His voice say to her, "Okay, well go in there and fix breakfast."

She said, "Lord, what do you mean go fix breakfast? I can't."

The Lord said to her, "What do you mean you can't? Yes, you can. I healed you, didn't I?"

She responded, "Well, yeah I guess so."

The Lord said, "Then get out of bed and go to your children. Go in there and see your family and cook them breakfast."

Suddenly, she swung one leg out of her bed. Then she swung her other leg out of the bed. Then she began to push herself up. She was surprised to find that she had strength in her legs. Then she began to put one leg in front of the other and she walked into the kitchen to see her family's shock, amazement, and exceeding joy. **It's a Miracle!"**

# NO DYING TODAY – NOT ON OUR WATCH

We pastored for several years before we became full time evangelist. There was a lady by the name of Frances in our church who had bad lung disease and was always on oxygen. I don't remember if it was COPD or some other lung disease. She knew her lungs were bad and should not be smoking, but she could not give up the cigarettes. We really worried about her a lot when she would be smoking round her oxygen.

But she would come to church every chance she got and was always asking for prayer for her family to get saved. She would sit at the back so she could step outside for a smoke. She loved being in the presence of the Lord and being in our church.

This one Sunday she had come back in from her smoke break coughing and choking. She sounded worse than we had ever heard her before. I realized something was wrong with her this Sunday. She was very sickly and frail. She could not sit up in the seat and she looked white as a ghost. I began to hear her making gurgle sounds and sometimes it seemed like she stopped breathing. Then all of sudden her head fell back, and her body went limp.

I told my husband, "Honey she is dying."

Both of us ran back to where she was, and we declared, "Not on our watch. You're not dying in this church. We're not going to have that on our record."

And we just began to pray and declare life in her body and in her lungs. We kept saying, "Frances, breathe in Jesus' name! You will live and not die in Jesus' name!"

We just kept praying and telling the church to help us pray. Suddenly, she gasps a deep breath and began to stir in her body, and we realized she started breathing. Praise God He heard our prayers and Frances did not die.

My husband was not raised around the supernatural. I am telling you this because it doesn't matter whether or not you've been raised in an atmosphere of **Miracle**s.

Some people have said to me, "The reason you and Randy see all of these **Miracle**s, is because your dad was Jack Coe."

And I tell them, "No, it's because Jesus Christ is the same yesterday, today, and forever."

You see, It is Jesus Christ that lives within you, the Holy Spirit, and the heavenly Father. People you come in contact with are going to have an encounter with God in you.

Jesus wants to use you to set people free. I want you to proclaim this loud and clear, "Those in my path are only a few feet from their **Miracle**."

Jesus told us in the book of Matthew that He has given us *"power over unclean spirits, to cast them out and to heal all sickness and disease."* (See

Matthew 10:1.) Do you believe what Jesus said? Jesus told us to lay hands on the sick, cast out devils, cleanse the lepers, and raise the dead. Freely we have received, and freely we should give. (See Matthew 10:8.) But you need to have a revelation of Who it is that lives inside of you.

Those who come across your pathway are only a few feet away from a **Miracle** if you but believe God. **"It's a Miracle!"**

# THE GIFTINGS OF GOD
## (Randy Herndon)

God gives many spiritual gifts to those who are born again and baptized in the Holy Spirit, but many times we do not discover these gifts because we are not pressing deeper into God. Now, I did not ask for the special gifts that God has given to me. I did not even know I had them until they began to be manifested. God just gave them to me. It was just like Christmas morning. And He handed me a package and I opened it.

God keeps doing wonderful things through my life, but it's also a little scary sometimes, because at times I will tell people the total opposite of what the medical profession is telling them. I'm not a doctor, nor have I studied anatomy. I am just listening to the Holy Spirit.

Here is a story about one time that the Holy Spirit spoke to me.

We were in a meeting in Media, Pennsylvania and I begin to share. I stood up and said, "There's someone here that is carrying their sickness like a badge of honor and God wants to heal you." I said, "Tonight, is your night to be healed and to be free."

I kept waiting for someone to respond because I knew I had heard from the Lord. Finally, a man came forward and I prayed for him. I knew God was setting him free. I didn't know his whole story and I didn't know what all was wrong, but I knew that this night was his night.

When we were back a year later, he told us his testimony. I had him to write his testimony down and give it to me. What you are about to read is this man's testimony in his own words.

"In 2005, I fought in the Iraq war as a combat infantry Sergeant. I was a machine gunner in the Gunner's turret of a Humvee Jeep. I was in the sunny triangle in a dangerous part of Iraq. There was nothing but insurgents and bad guys around us. I did about 200 combat missions in a nine-month period.

The last three months of my tour, I was assigned to a desk job. However, let me just say that I used my weapon. I have never liked it when people ask me if I killed anyone because it is personal. All I can say is that I saw and experienced a lot of horrible things.

When I came home, I was diagnosed with PTSD and that means post-traumatic stress disorder. During World War II, this was called shell shock. And then in Korea and Vietnam, it was called flashbacks.

Now it's called PTSD. From 2005 to about 2015, I suffered with terrible nightmares. I would wake up in the middle of the night, screaming, cursing, shouting, and punching my pillow. I would be completely covered in sweat.

During these nightmares I would scare my wife almost every single time, but she loves me so much that she would comfort me, instead of quitting on me or giving up on me. You could say that she was my rock during those times. Sometimes my nightmares would be a weird mix of what I saw in Iraq and my current life issues. And I'll give you an example. I used to have this reoccurring nightmare. It went something like this.

I am in a building and in a combat situation. Now this was a strange deal because I never went into clear buildings of the enemy, because I was a machine gunner, and I was in the Turret of a Humvee. I was standing by with my machine guns, in the turret, pulling security while the ground troops cleared rooms and buildings. So, the dream continues.

I could hear a soldier screaming for help. 'Save me, save me!'

191

I would run over and turn the soldier over. In this dream this soldier always was my dad bleeding to death. My dad died in 2011 from a stroke so these nightmares did not make sense at all. It truly was the devil tormenting me. I found myself unconsciously bragging about my condition to people. Whenever I would talk to people about my service in Iraq, they would ask me if I was okay. And I said, 'Well, yeah, sure.'

I'm okay. I have PTSD. But you know, that is expected. I was almost wearing my PTSD as a badge of honor, puffing my chest out about having PTSD, like it was some sort of a cool thing that only combat guys get. Let me tell you, there's nothing cool about PTSD.

Then Randy and Joanna Herndon came into my life. It was around 2015 when they came to our church, Randy got up at one of the healing services and said, 'There is someone here who has a medical condition. You're almost accepting this condition as a kind of, I don't know, wearing it like a badge of honor or something like that. And I'm here to tell you that Jesus doesn't want you to have any pain or suffering. You are not meant to wear an ailment or a condition as a badge of honor. If you want to be truly free from this tonight, then I'm encouraging you to come on down and be set free'

I was sitting in the congregation thinking, 'Oh my God, he's talking to me!' I felt God nudge me to come down to the altar and I did. Randy prayed for me. As he prayed for me, I accepted what he prayed, and at that moment I was completely and totally set free from all my nightmares immediately. Since that day, I have not had a single nightmare at all. Not one more PTSD nightmare. Plus, no other kinds of nightmares.

It has been about six years now, and I have been nightmare free. And I know it's God. Yet I do want to thank God for the Herndon's in this, because they were the instruments that God used to heal me. It is hard to explain to people or for them to imagine how much I suffered because of these terrible horrifying nightmares. Had God not used them pray over me, I am not sure what would have happened to me. I am nightmare free."

That story was cool but what is neat about this is that ever since this happened, I have been sharing this story, and other veterans will now come up and get prayed for. The Lord told me that I needed to share this more and more. Now I understand why. God is healing veterans and others from PTSD. **"It's a Miracle"**

## HEALED OF DIABETES BY DIVINE DIRECTION
### (Randy Herndon)

I was in a church where we were praying for people in a prayer line, a lady walked up and said "I want off my medicine. I want to be healed tonight."

When I looked at her God gave me a word of knowledge for her. I said, "You have diabetes."

She said, "Yes, I do, and I'm tired of taking this medicine. I want to be healed."

I said, "You need to wait two years. And after that two-year period, God's going to heal you. You need to continue your medicine and in one year they will lower your medicine. During this two-year period, they will drop your medicine down some more. At the end of two years, they will take you off the medicine because you will be healed of diabetes."

She said, "Okay."

I walked off and started praying for somebody else thinking all along there is no way this woman will go and wait two years. But two years later, Joanna was in a meeting ministering, and out of the blue this woman I had spoken over came up to her.

She asked Joanna, "Where's your husband? I need to give him a testimony. I want to tell him what he told me came to pass." Then she started telling Joanna about the two-year prophetic word that I gave her. She said, "Tell Randy it was two years to the day that I received that word that my diabetes left." She said, "I didn't do anything in between. I didn't try to get rid of my medicine. I just stayed on my normal routine, followed the doctor's advice, and today I'm healed."

What is amazing to me is that someone would have the intestinal fortitude to wait two years and trust God that long. Come to find out, she was a pastor of a local church not too far from the place where we prayed for her. **"It's a Miracle!"**


## IT'S STRANGE HOW GOD WORKS
### (Randy Herndon)

I want to share with you about an amazing healing, but how the Lord brought it about is strange. You see, every time we minister healing, we need to hear from God. Throughout Scripture, Jesus did many different things for people which brought about their healing.

The heavenly Father, in one instance, had Jesus' spit in the dirt and make mud, then He put it on a blind man's eyes and told him to go wash. When the blind man washed, his eyes were opened. Another time He had a dumb man stick out his tongue, then Jesus' spit on it and the dumb man could speak.

Now, this healing testimony takes place in Ashland, Virginia at Ruth Heflin's camp. They have three to four meetings a day there at Calvary Pentecostal Tabernacle. We were at one meeting when a lady walked up and tapped me on the shoulder.

She asked, "Would you pray for my son?"

I said, "Well, sure. We will pray for him in the prayer lines tonight if that's okay?"

I had never seen this woman in my life before this incident. This was during the time when Joanna was one of the speakers at the camp. They knew us from the ministry and because we had been there praying for people in the prayer lines.

Joanna was praying for this lady who said her ankles hurt and she couldn't stand on her feet long. She missed dancing in worship because she was in so much pain. Joanna prayed for her, and her ankles stopped hurting.

She said, "This is great, but I wasn't coming for myself or expecting this, **Miracle**. We brought our son and wanted you to pray for him. I asked your husband today if y'all could pray for him tonight?"

"Yes, we can pray for him. Where is he?" Joanna asked her.

She turned to get him, and Joanna started praying for someone else so I said, "Bring him over here, I will pray for him."

Now at the campground in Ashland, there's a little concrete platform back behind where we were praying. So, I took this boy over to this concrete wall and had him sit down. This young man was between the age of 14 to 15 years old.

It turns out that he had never played sports. He loved sports and he wanted to play but he'd never been able to because there was something wrong with his leg and it never worked properly. The medical professionals did not know what the problem was. A doctor's appointment had been set up in the next few days after returning from the camp to do exploratory surgery.

Now, I did not have a clue about what was going on, I was just following the Holy Spirit. You might say I was just going with my gut feeling. I heard myself telling him to put the heel of his foot into my hand.

After I had ahold of his heel, I thought 'Okay, Lord, what do I do now?'

I heard the voice of the Lord say, "Pull really hard!" So, I pulled hard.

Amazingly when I did, we all heard a loud pop. Not only did I hear this pop, but I also felt it in his leg. To be honest with you, at the time it scared me to death.

I looked up at him and I said, "You, okay?"

He says, "Oh yeah, feels great."

I said, "Well, stand up." He stood up and I said, "You need to walk." He started walking, but he still had a limp. I said, "Oh, wait a minute, wait a minute, come back over here. What's wrong?"

He said, "It's not my leg now, it's my foot."

Now, at that moment I felt like Joe, the super

Christian. I said, "Get back here and sit on this wall. Now give me that other foot."

So then he stuck the other leg up. Now I went to do exactly what I did with the other foot when I sensed I needed to do something different. I had him take his shoe off and then his sock. Then he put his heel into my hand like before. I looked at his foot in my hand. I found myself grabbing all his toes. I kept pulling back and forth on his toes speaking in tongues the whole time. When I was done, I said, "How does that feel?"

He goes, "Oh man, it feels great!" And he got up and started to run off again.

I shouted at him and said, "Whoa, stop! Hey, what was wrong with your foot?"

He said, "I had four broken toes."

My heart went up in my throat because I knew what I had just done to his foot. I asked him later when I was able to speak to him again, "When did your toes get healed in this process that I was taking you through?"

He said, "The second you put your hands on my toes, I could feel them being healed."

The next day we were going to a meeting, and he came up to us all covered in sweat. Here he had been out playing basketball for the very first time that he has ever played in his life.

He said, "Thank y'all so much."

Of course, we told him that we did not heal him. Only Jesus Christ can heal, and He is the Great Physician. **"It's a Miracle!"**

## OPEN VISION BRINGS A HEALING
### (Randy Herndon)

We were in Richmond, Virginia having healing meetings. There were lots of healings and **Miracle**s happening there. This is one of my favorite stories to tell about a woman that we ministered too. We had finished preaching and we had prayed for lots of the people that were present. We were sitting down, and this lady came up to me. She was an older lady and I discovered later that she was in her seventies.

She came up and very politely asked me if I could pray for her. I said, "Well, sure. Do you mind if I sit down here for a few minutes? I'm a little tired."

"Not at all," she responded.

After I rested a little bit, I got up and I was going to put my hands on her to pray. I had almost laid my hands upon her when out of my mouth came these words, "What's wrong with your windpipe?"

She said, "I'm having trouble breathing. I am supposed to go to the doctor to be examined and do certain test to find out what is wrong."

I said, "I see it."

This is one of the first few times I first started seeing inside bodies. This is something that the Lord shows me sometimes. I cannot fully explain it to you, but when the Lord shows me, I let people know and I pray for them. I try to relay things I see to help people understand, because I'm not a doctor and I don't know anatomy very well, but I'm learning more and more with the Lord's help.

What I saw in this lady was like a garden hose when it's twisted. Now most people know if you twist a garden hose that you cannot get water to run through it. Her air was constricted in her windpipe the same way.

While I was praying for her, I saw it start to untwist and loosen up. Then I saw that it was completely clear to where air could flow through it normally.

I said, "You need to take a deep breath."

She begins to take shallow breaths like she's been used to doing. I said again, "Take a deep breath!" She's not used to taking a deep breath because she had not been able to for a long time. She once again just took small shallow breaths. But then I jumped up and I said in a commanding tone, "Take a deep breath!" When I jumped up and commanded her to take a deep breath, it scared her, and without thinking she took a real deep breath. When she did, her whole countenance changed. At that moment she realized that she could breathe deep, and she was healed.

She absolutely went crazy for Jesus Christ and started to dance around like a teenager. She began to declare loudly and boldly, "The Lord has healed me."

The next day, as we were at the hotel packing our bags to get ready to head out of Richmond, we got a call from the pastor, and he told us that this woman was his mom. The pastor said, "I would like to ask you to stay longer, if you are available. There have been lots of **Miracle**s and healings. People are telling others, and more people want to come."

We stayed and extended the meetings. God continued to heal, save, deliver, and set people free. **"It's a Miracle!"**

# RICHARD, RICHARD, RICHARD
### (Randy Herndon)

We were in Mount Holly Springs, Pennsylvania, and we were praying for people in the prayer line. Joanna was praying for someone, and this other man was standing in the prayer line.

After he got prayer, he kept standing there because he wanted to talk to the pastor. I heard him talking to the pastor and he was talking about something job related; but I didn't know what they were saying.

I kept hearing the name, Richard, over and over and over. It just wouldn't leave me alone. I said, "Lord, am I supposed to speak this name to this man? What is the deal here?" I finally got up after curiosity got me. I walked over to him, and I said, "Do you know a man named Richard?"

He says, "Yes, Richard is my boss's name."

He was waiting for me to tell him something more, but I didn't have anything else. I told him I would pray and see if the Lord would give me something else about Richard or why Richard.

So, he went and sat down in the back of the church. Well, I begin to inquire of the Lord, "Tell me what else. Why are you telling me about Richard?"

Now Joanna had heard the man talking to the pastor and how he was worried about his job. He had been asking the pastor and the church to pray about what was going on at his job. He was asking the pastor if the Lord had showed him anything. The pastor said he hadn't heard or felt anything from the Lord.

I said, "Lord, what is this about Richard?"

Suddenly, I hear the Lord say, "You go tell that man that Richard speaks out of both sides of his mouth, and not to trust him."

I went back and told him exactly what the Lord

spoke to me. He looked like I'd slapped him in the face. Well, come to find out later, Richard, his boss, told him that he would be okay in his job. He thought Richard was his friend and was helping him keep his job, but not too long after this Richard fired him. But because the word of the Lord had come to me for him, it did not devastate him like it otherwise would have. How did this come to me? With just one word: Richard.

# IT HAPPENED IN 3 DAYS
## (Randy Herndon)

We were in the nation of Colombia, South America. We were headed to a meeting that was up in the mountains. We drove two hours or more to get up into the mountains. Colombia's temperatures are usually 85 to 87 degrees every day. Of course, with the humidity it feels like high 90s. But up in the mountains it was cool.

I said, "Yeah, I love this. This is great."

We were going to a house meeting at Pastor Diego's house. He has a weekly house meeting outside on his patio. So, I'm thinking, 'Oh, this is going to be cool.' The pastor had a nice house up in the mountain. It was also nice being outside.

When we arrived at this pastor's house, we discovered that he spoke English. He told me, "Hey, listen, I told this lady that is a couple of houses down from here that y'all were coming, and that y'all could pray for her. I think she has cancer, but I'm not 100% sure about all that. I've invited her to come to our meeting today. She has her two sisters in town that have come to visit her. I told her to bring them too. I hope all three of them will come."

So, we talked back and forth until the service started. There was about thirty or more people out there on his patio during praise and worship. Now, I was looking for these three people to arrive at any moment as praise and worship was going on. Suddenly these three ladies came walking into the front gate. You could tell the one in the middle was extremely sick. I leaned over to Pastor Diego, and I said, "Pastor, is that them?"

He replied, "Yes, and she is the one in the middle."

"Okay." I said to the pastor, "Would it be okay if we pray for her right now?"

He said, "Sure," and he got up and stopped the praise and worship service so I could pray for them.

The ladies came up front and I walked up to where they were at. I was simply going to do what Joanna and I have done through the years. We were going to lay hands on her in the traditional way according to the Scriptures. Well, I got almost to putting my hands on her head when the Lord stopped me.

He said, "Tell her this, "You have a sore on your

body about the size of the palm of my hand. It will not heal. And I'm telling you today that in three days, this thing will scab over and fall off in your bed."

I told her exactly what the Lord told me and then I thought, "What did you just tell her?!" You know, the natural kicks in; but we're not operating in the natural, we're operating in the supernatural.

So, I go to put my hand on her head again and the Lord stopped me again. He said, "Tell her this!"

What I see now is strange. I'm seeing inside her body. Her upper body, from her waist up looked like two trees with many branches, but no leaves.

I said, "Lord, what am I seeing?"

He said, "That's cancer!" The moment I heard the word cancer, it turned snow white in front of my eyes.

I said, "Lord, what are you doing now?"

He said, "I'm killing it at the root."

Suddenly, I back off, and I tell her all this. Of course, we did not see any change immediately.

You must remember that just because we don't see something happen in the natural does not mean God is not doing it. Many times, we have prayed for people and left town, and not heard about the **Miracle**s God did for those we prayed for until later.

Joanna and I were in Colombia for about a month ministering at many different locations. It was so glorious because we saw God do many wonderful things.

About two weeks after we had ministered at Pastor Diego's house, we received an email from him. He said, "I have good news and bad news." He said, "Remember the woman you said that had a sore on her body? You told her that it would fall off in her bed in three days. Well, it happened just like you said it would. That's the good news."

As I continue reading the e-mail I'm thinking, 'Ok now, that was the good news. Oh no, now what is the bad news? Did she die?'

But Pastor Diego said she had gone into surgery and was cut open. The people that were surrounding this woman put a lot of pressure on her to go to the hospital and have this cancer cut out. She argued with them because she felt good, and the sore healed in 3 days, but the doctors made her do the surgery. They got her in the operating room. They cut this poor woman open and could not find any cancer anywhere in her body. They declared that she was cancer free! The bad news was that she had to go through a major operation for nothing. **"It's a Miracle!"**

# AMERICAN AIRLINES EMPLOYEE
# RECEIVES A MIRACLE
### (Randy Herndon)

The last week we were in Colombia I got sick. We were about three days from leaving and our interpreter came out and said, "Randy, if you go to the airport and you act sick, they are not going to let you leave."

I said, "Andy, watch me. I can act."

We went to the airport. Well, when they check your bags, they do it all outside. It's very hot and steamy. I was sitting out there, sweating, and so sick.

This guard looked over at me and motioned that he wanted to check my baggage. He was a customs agent. I said, "Okay, so here we go."

Well, he came over and opened my suitcase. He didn't bother with Joanna's at all. He looked at mine and he pulled out a generic cheap bottle of aspirin, like one you buy at Walgreens or Walmart. When he found this bottle of aspirins, he began to shake it at me and speak something in Spanish.

I kept telling him, "It's aspirin. You can have them if you want them. I don't care. I can buy another bottle for two dollars." But of course, he didn't understand a single thing I was saying. So finally, he threw it back into my suitcase, and let me go.

It looked like we were going to have to go back to the end of the line; but praise God, this man put us at the front counter. We got inside where it was air conditioned, but there was another checkpoint we had to go through.

I was right by our gate looking at our American Airlines flight for home. I noticed before we could board the plane, they had to do another baggage check. I was thinking, 'How many times are they going to do this?'

Remember now, I was sick, so I was thinking, 'Why can't we just go and sit down somewhere? I feel like I am going to throw up at any moment.'

They finally allowed us to go into the boarding area. I was getting close to the plane. I could see that American Airlines jet and I go, "Yeah, baby, I'm on my way home one way or another."

I was so sick and so ready to get home, but I was also wondering if we even made much difference in this country.

So, we're sitting there waiting. Joanna went to get come coffee and when she came back, there was a young lady that came out of a side door with an American Airlines uniform on. She kept walking towards me. I thought she was headed to the flight desk, but she came over and she introduced herself to us. She said, "Do you remember me?"

Of course, we had seen thousands of people during

our time in Colombia. I said, "Well, honestly, I don't sweetheart, would you remind us?"

She said, "I was at the youth meeting at the Nazarene church that you both spoke at and prayed for people. I told you both I had breast cancer in both breasts. You asked me how old I was. I'm twenty-two. You both told me I was too young for that to be happening to me. Then you both prayed for me. When I saw you here at the airport, I had to make my way to find you and let you know I just came back from the doctor yesterday, they said they cannot find the cancer. It was gone!!"

That was a wonderful testimony to hear as we were boarding the airplane to come back to America. In fact, she said, "Grab your bags and follow me." She took us past the last custom check point and put us on the airplane first. **"It's a Miracle!"**

# IT'S A MIRACLE

# CHAPTER EIGHT
## PROFESSIONALS ASKING QUESTIONS

The next year I went to Colombia without Randy. I went back to Pastor Diego's house where that amazing **Miracle** happened with the lady who was healed of cancer. When I arrived back at Pastor Diego's house for the meeting, I was surprised to find a doctor, a caregiver, and a lawyer there waiting for me.

They were asking Diego, "Where are the people who were involved in that **Miracle** last year?"

Diego said, "Well, the wife is here but the husband did not come." They were looking for Randy.

I said, "He didn't come with me this year." They insisted that they needed to speak to him. They had briefcases and notebooks. I said, "I'm sorry, he's not here. What do you need to know?"

They said, "We want to know what he did? How he healed that lady of cancer? What is his method?"

I don't know if they thought we had a special formula. I think they thought that if we had a secret formula, and they could get their hands on it, that they would be very wealthy men. They knew that this lady had cancer, and somehow all the cancer was now gone. So, they were there with their pens and paper trying to get information. They told me that they needed to speak to him even if it was just by phone. They insisted we must talk to him.

I said, "Well, I can't help you right now. We're fixing to start a meeting, but I can tell you that it wasn't him."

They asked, "Who did it then?"

I said, "I know who done it, but it wasn't my husband. It was another physician. It was Doctor Jesus!"

"Who?"

I said, "Doctor Jesus."

"Well, where is He?" they asked.

I said, "Well, if you'll stay for the service, He will be here."

They said, "Well, we want to talk to somebody." So, they stayed.

I said, "I'll talk to you more after the service."

Well, the service began, and here sat the caregiver, the lawyer, and the doctor. God began to move during that meeting. After I preached, I began to pray for the people.

There was a man there who was in a wheelchair. I think he had muscular dystrophy, because his muscles were all shrinking, and his head was flopped back. He had a caregiver with him who was working with him. I went over to where he was sitting in his wheelchair.

As I was praying for this man, I said, "Sir, you're a pastor and God's not through with you yet."

I am sure that the three professionals were sitting there thinking, 'What in the world is she talking about?' The man in the wheelchair was almost incapable of doing anything. I mean, he could move his hand a little bit, but he had no control over any other part of his body.

After I gave this gentleman that prophetic word he began to cry. He began to respond by struggling to say, "Thank you!"

I said, "God's not through with you yet, and the enemy's trying to stop you. But God said, 'You will get up and you will finish what He gave you to finish. It will be completed.'"

I found out later that he had been a pastor of a church when he was struck with this infirmity. The caregiver who was with this pastor dropped to the floor and started weeping and crying. The pastor's wife went to the floor on her knees weeping and crying as well because she knew that everything, I was telling him was so accurate.

Now remember, I did not have any information about him, I just had a word of knowledge about his situation.

Not everything manifested right then and there, but we did begin to see it change immediately. His head, which was completely drooped over, began to come up. Then he began to move other parts of his body which he was not capable of when he first came to the meeting. Oh, how I wanted to see him get up out of that wheelchair, but it didn't happen in that moment. However, we did see two very evident **Miracle**s happening in his body.

Then I turned to a man sitting near him who had to use special metal crutches. He had some type of metal support system wrapped around his forearm to brace him. I prayed for this man, and I said, "God, you bring these hips into alignment." I do not remember exactly everything I said but I know that God was moving mightily as I prayed.

Suddenly, the crutches went flying and the man went to walking. The lawyer, caretaker, and doctor who were there, began to quickly and furiously write down everything they saw.

At the back of Pastor Diego's patio there was a little boy laying on a bed. This little boy might have been about two years old. He had his own private nurse standing over him and two other people standing beside him. I noticed these three professionals who came to talk to Randy were following me around the place while I was praying for different ones. I stopped at this baby boy and asked what was wrong and why he was laying there so lifeless.

"Is this baby in a coma?" I asked.

They told me a sad story. This little boy had swallowed a grape and it got caught in his windpipe. It cut off his oxygen supply to where he could not breathe. By the time they were able to remove the grape, he already had too much damage to the brain. They had to put this tube in him to breathe, and it turned him into almost a vegetable state. The doctor said that there was major brain damage, and the boy would never be normal. From all the indications, the boy had died, and the doctors brought him back to life.

I began to pray for this baby in the name of Jesus. As I was praying over him, suddenly his eyes popped open, and he began to look around everywhere. I said to this little child, "Hello sweetie, can you see me?"

This little boy looked toward me and smiled. He kept turning his head and looking around like he just woke up. The nurse who had been watching over this little boy looked so surprised. The nurse began to check his vitals and shined a flashlight into his eyes. Those who were there with the boy got extremely excited.

I didn't know what they were saying because I do not speak Spanish, but I asked them if this had happened previously where the child would respond and look around.

They said, "No, he has never done this since the day he went into a coma."

The next thing I knew, the area grew crowded.

Here was the doctor, the lawyer, and the other caregiver, and those who were with the boy and others were all close by. Everyone was talking so fast in Spanish. I knew they were excited.

The three professionals were there with their papers and pens, writing as fast as they could and asking questions.

I asked my interpreter what was going on. He said, "They are all surprised and excited that the boy is back."

I didn't know everything they were asking because I had more people to pray for, but my interpreter said the professionals wanted to know if the boy was really in coma or just asleep and I woke him up. They were all in shock and amazement.

God just showed up and showed them who Doctor Jesus was. They had encountered Doctor Jesus for themselves by witnessing **Miracle** after **Miracle** in this meeting. There were many **Miracle**s that happened in that house that night because Jesus showed up.

The pastor who was in the wheelchair was getting better by the minute. He began to be able to move his hands in ways that he had not done previously.

The pastor's wife was so excited that she kept on declaring, "God's doing it, God's doing it."

This pastor's caregiver was so overwhelmed by what was happening that he kept on passing out, coming to, and passing out again. It must have been four or five times that he went to the floor. I discovered later that the caregiver used to go to this pastor's church. He became a nurse to help his pastor through this difficult time.

Randy and I never got to fully find out what all the three professionals wanted. I didn't know if they came because they lost money since there was no cancer left in their patient from last year, because she was a very wealthy lady. Maybe they could be wanting to see if Randy had a cure for cancer and get information about this cure so they could get rich themselves. We didn't have any idea why they were there.

No matter what they encountered and experienced that night, Doctor Jesus was working in the lives and hearts of people. Some people even gave their hearts to Jesus Christ that night.

The woman who had an incurable case of cancer is still alive to this day. According to the experts, she was supposed to be dead, but Doctor Jesus said, "You will live and not die, and declare the glories of God." **"It's a Miracle!"**


## STRANGE AND AMAZING HEALING FROM BREAST CANCER
### (Randy Herndon)

Have you ever been in a healing line or in a church and watched people being prayed for, and somebody in that line will say, "I'm healed," and not a soul touched them or prayed for them? I mean, have you been there? Isn't that unbelievable? That should tell us who is doing the healing.

We were in upstate New York. Syracuse, I believe. Joanna had just preached a wonderful message. We prayed for everybody who wanted prayer, and I sat down. One of the young ladies came off the platform that was in the praise and worship team. She approached me in a very hesitant way. She said to me very softly, "I know you must be tired praying for all these people, but would you mind praying for me?"

I said, "Well, of course I'll pray for you. You've been up there singing and playing all this time, why don't you just go ahead and have a seat and let me stand up and pray for you."

She was very grateful because she was a little tired at the time. They had been ministering in music for a long time. So she sat down, and as my custom is, I was going to lay hands on her. I got about six inches away from her with my hands, and the Lord stopped me. The Lord said to me, "Tell her this." I pointed my finger at her and said, "You have breast cancer."

She looked up at me like I had slapped her across the face. She said, "How did you know that? Nobody knows that, not even my husband."

Her husband was sitting right next to her when I told her that so, I thought, 'Well he knows now.'

I said, "All right, now listen to me, this is going to sound strange. I see this thing and it's in your right breast. It's about the size of my thumb, and the end of it looks like tentacles." That's all I could say.

And then Joanna said, "Well, there's a dry erase board behind you. Why don't you just draw a picture of it."

I got up, and I drew it in detail. After I had

explained what this growth looked like, out of my mouth came this. I said, "I see this cancer moving out of your right breast and into your left breast. It will then come out of your left breast and hover in mid-air and then just disappear. It will not leave a hole or a scar."

Now, that sounds like a fairy tale, doesn't it? It doesn't sound like what happens in the natural world. You must realize we're dealing in the supernatural.

Of course, after I told her this, she looked at me like I had just landed on the earth from a spaceship from Mars.

I said, "Now I told you from the beginning this was going to be on the strange side. So don't worry about this."

Well, we found out later that she fought her family, the medical profession, and friends that were constantly insisting that she get something done about the cancer in her breast. Every time she saw her doctor, she would tell him what I had told her, but he would just laugh her off and tell her the cancer was still there. He kept insisting she needed to get it cut out.

For eight long months she told him, "No I am not doing anything." She just kept standing on the word and saying, "That man told me that I would be healed of this. I'm standing on God's word." The cancer did not grow or shrink.

Well, a year later, we came back to minister in that church, and they told us the amazing story of what happened to her. People put so much pressure on her that she finally said, "Okay, fine. I'll go to the hospital and get it cut out."

They prepped her for the operation by putting black marks where they were going to have to go in and remove this growth. Right before they operated, the doctor said, "I want to reconfirm exactly what we're doing. Just lay right here and I'm going to check the machines."

Now, she had told the doctor what I had said to her several times each visit. Of course, the doctor thought that she was dealing with someone who was just a religious nut. The doctor was gone for a very long time but finally came back into the operating room with a very weird and strange look on his face.

The doctor looked at her and said, "Get your clothes on and meet me in my office."

She was thinking, "What in the world is going on now?" But she got dressed, and she went to his office.

He looked at her and he said, "Tell me what that man said to you exactly. You know that preacher who told you about what he saw with the cancer." She tells him and he said, "Tell me again!" She tells him again. He said, "Tell me again." For the third time, she tells him again.

She said, "Okay, what's going on?"

He said, "Well, I was checking my machines. I saw this cancer moving out of your right breast, into your left breast. Then I saw it move out of your breast, and it was hovering in the air. It looked so real to me that I grabbed at it with my hand, and it disappeared. Now I'm studying the machine and can't find it anywhere. We cannot operate because I can't find it!"

But that is not all the story, the doctor was a Muslim. What did he just see? He saw a divine **Miracle** right in front of his eyes that he could not deny. The wonderful news is that this doctor got gloriously saved and filled with the Holy Spirit. The Lord made a believer out of him on that day. He is serving the Lord at this very moment. **"It's A Miracle!"**

## A WOMAN HEALED OF BREAST CANCER

My husband, Randy, prayed for a lady with breast cancer in Richmond, Virginia when we were there for a few days ministering. This lady was extremely scared and desperate because she had received the bad report of having breast cancer. She had heard our testimony in one of our meetings about the woman who was healed from cancer in Colombia. We also had shared about the woman who was healed from the breast cancer in New York.

She came up to us during the time of prayer in one of the meetings she was attending. Tears were rolling down her face. She walked right up to my husband, and she said, "I have cancer in my breast." She said, "Please, would you please, please pray for me?"

Randy said, "Sure."

She said, "I believe that if you pray for me that I'll be healed. Like those two stories you told us tonight, the doctors have told me that they cannot do anything to save my breast. They told me they're going to take my breast off. Even if they take my breast, they told me there's no guarantee that I will be able to survive this cancer."

Randy began to pray over her in the name of Jesus. Suddenly he stopped. He said, "I believe God is killing this cancer at its root right now!"

She said, "Oh, really? That's what I was praying he would do for me like he did for those others you prayed for."

He said, "I believe it, and I'm going to believe it for you. He told her that the doctors would not do any surgery or be able to find cancer."

It was sometime later before we saw her again when we were back in the area. The pastor of the church that we had ministered in wanted us to come back because so many **Miracle**s had happened there.

This precious sister, who they said had cancer in her breast, showed up at one of our meetings. She'd just been to the doctor and had test after test from the medical world. They told her that they could not find any cancer in her breast. She told them that she wanted that in writing. She came running into the service waving her paper from the doctor. She was shouting and praising God, "Look here, look here."

Randy said, "Look at what?"

"I have no cancer. I told them I wanted them to put it in writing. And all they could write on my file was **'It's a Miracle!'** The cancer is gone!"

They said, "Now we still need to check you in a year." They checked her a year later, and it was still gone. They checked her the following year, and there still was no cancer.

Jesus Christ is the same yesterday, today and forever. If He did it before, He will do it again. **"It's a Miracle!"**

## GOD HEALS A PASTOR'S LUNGS
### (Randy Herndon)

We were in Cleveland, Tennessee at the UCCMA conference, which was H Richard Hall's organization. My wife was one of the speakers. Several pastor friends heard she was speaking there, so some called to inquire, and some showed up. Dr. T.L. Lowrey and Pastor Greg Casto both called and came to see us.

The people at the conference were so excited that Dr. T.L. Lowery was coming to the meeting to see us. They did not realize that he and his wife, Mildred, were our friends. We were so excited to see everyone and to reconnect.

There were others that came, but this one pastor friend came because he needed a healing. His name was Pastor David Woodrow, who has since gone home to be with the Lord.

I went up to Pastor David, looked at him and I said, "David, what's wrong with you?"

He said, "I've got walking pneumonia."

I said, "I can see something." I put my hands on his chest where his lungs were. The minute I put my hands on his chest the Holy Spirit was showing me his lungs. I saw that his lungs were funnel shaped. They were wide at the top but got narrow at the bottom. This was the case in both lungs. Then I saw ring like streaks of light going up and down in his lungs. They just kept going up and down. I was thinking, 'Lord, what are you doing?'

I heard the Lord say, "I'm healing his lungs." It was obvious that the Holy Spirit was moving upon Pastor David's body, so I left him there in the hands of the Lord and I went down and started praying for other people who needed a healing.

It was not very long before Pastor David came over to me and tapped me on the shoulder. He said, "I feel great. What did you do?"

I said, "All I did was pray, David. God did the rest."

The next day David called us and told us he felt so good, and his lungs were so clear that he worked out in his garden all day and was going to shower and come see us again at the conference. Sometimes it's just that simple. Just lay your hands on them. **"It's a Miracle!**

# A NURSE EXPERIENCES A MIRACLE
## (Randy Herndon)

We were in Nanticoke, Pennsylvania. We had quite a good number of people who came up front to get prayed for. Sometimes Joanna and I split up to pray for people and sometimes we do it together. In this meeting we were praying together. We decided to start on the far end of this prayer line. We were both together at the one end praying, and Joanna took off toward the other end of the line, so I followed.

As I was walking past all these people, suddenly I heard the Holy Spirit say, "Stop!" So I stopped. Joanna didn't even know I had stopped, she just kept on walking.

As I turned, I ended up looking right at a particular lady. I looked at the lady and said, "What's wrong with your shoulders?"

Her eyes got really big. "How did you know?" she asked.

I said, "I don't know anything, honey, except the Holy Spirit told me to stop and pray for your shoulders."

She said, "Well, I don't have any cartilage in either one of my rotator cuffs."

I began to pray for this lady. Now mind you, I'm not praying big flowery, long prayers. No, not at all.

The word of God gives us instructions on how to pray. Jesus said to speak to the mountain, and it would be removed. We are told to call those things which are not, as though they were.

After I prayed for this lady I said, "Now do what you could not do before."

She began to move her arms and shoulders all around, up and down, front and back. She had not been able to raise her hands over her head and now was doing that too. She started laughing hysterically.

I'm thinking, 'Okay, that's cool, I'll laugh too.' I asked her if there was a reason why she was laughing so much.

She said, "Yes, I am a nurse and I have to lift people all day long. Everyone at work knows how bad my condition is. I can't wait to go show the nurses and doctors what God has done for me."

You know, it's fun to watch God heal people that are hurting. It's so fun to me. I love it when God does that. This lady was going to be a witness to all those people in that hospital. "It's a Miracle!"

# PASTOR'S DAD HEALED
## (Randy Herndon)

We were in Richmond, Virginia with Bishop Husband. He pastored in an older church building that had a high cathedral ceiling, stained glass windows and one of those great big steeples. It was a beautiful old church. I love seeing the beautiful craftsmanship of these older church buildings.

During ministry time, there were people getting healed in their backs, knees, and necks, and from headaches, and other things. The people would get excited about their healing and would take off running around the sanctuary, and around the altar area where we were praying. Some of them were jumping up and down.

The pastor walked over to me, and leaned over, and he said, "Hey, would you pray for my father?"

I said, "Yes, what's wrong with him?"

He told me, "He has trouble with his knees. He wears these knee braces, and he is also diabetic."

I said, "Well sure, bring him up here."

The pastor got his dad to come to the front and I took him over to a front pew to have him sit down. He was wearing a black suit and was dressed like a preacher. I found out later he was a Baptist but came to this Pentecostal church because his son was the pastor.

I said, "Why don't you sit down here and let me put my hands on you."

As I laid my hands upon him, and prayed over him, he spoke up. "What is that? What are you doing to me?" Both of his knees started getting hot.

I said, "The Lord's healing your knees." He stood up as if to leave, and I said, "Well, wait a minute, don't you have sugar diabetes?"

"Yeah," he said.

I said, "Well, let me pray for that". So I prayed for that sugar diabetes to be gone.

He started lifting his legs up and down. He sat down, then got back up and began to walk around. I had already gone on to pray for someone else, but I noticed this happening with my peripheral vision. I looked over, and here the pastor's dad was pulling his pants legs up. My wife thought he was pulling off his clothes and looked away quickly, but he wasn't. He was unsnapping and unbuckling the braces that were on his legs. He finally got the braces off and pulled his pant legs back down.

Now the pastor's father was in his 70s, but you sure couldn't tell it by the way he started acting. Before we knew what he was doing he took off running. He ran to the center of the church, where Joanna was standing, and threw the braces up into the air to where they looked like they were going to hit that high ceiling. They fell back to the floor almost hitting Joanna. He took off running again, just like everyone else did. He was running all over the church. His knees were completely healed and strong.

We found out later he was healed of diabetes that night too. He went home that night and started eating ice cream and donuts and all the stuff he couldn't eat before.

His wife tried to stop him and told him, "You need to still watch yourself."

He told her, "No, I'm healed."

He went back to the doctor, and they verified that he was no longer a diabetic. This older gentleman went back to his home church to tell his pastor and the congregation that they needed to start preaching on healing because it was for real. Jesus still heals today. **"It's a Miracle!"**

# SHE HAD ONLY ONE KIDNEY

There was a **Miracle** in California that Linda, a friend of ours, prayed for. A lady named Michele told Linda that she only had one kidney.

She said, "I need a **Miracle** because my only good kidney is getting worse. They say if it continues to get worse, I'm not going to be able to function very well with one kidney. You see, I gave one of my good kidneys to someone who needed it."

After praying for her, she went back to the doctors. The doctors were absolutely amazed because her one kidney was now operating like two kidneys in one. **"It's a Miracle!"**

## ANOTHER KIDNEY MIRACLE

Now I'm in Myakka, Florida and a woman came crying to me to please pray. "I need a **Miracle**," she said, "my kidneys are bad and if they continue to get worse, I will have to go on dialysis." She said her count was 17 and if she dropped to 14, she would have to be put on dialysis.

I told her of the story of the **Miracle** that God did with the lady in California who only had one kidney. I said, "I believe if God can do that for her, He can heal your kidneys and you will not have to go on dialysis." I laid hands on her and begin to tell the Lord how He did it for Michele in California, and would He do a **Miracle** for this lady in Florida.

I prayed, "In the name of Jesus be healed."

Now did not see any change in her, but we had meetings for several nights there. The last night she testified that the doctor's report came back, and her kidney levels had gone up from 17 to 34. The doctor told her that that doesn't happen, but it showed to be improving and the doctor was amazed. The doctor told her it was a **Miracle**. **"It's a Miracle!"**

# A MIRACLE FOR THE UNBELIEVER

**(Randy Herndon)**

We were in a service in Pittston, Pennsylvania. There was an older man who came to the meeting with his son. I noticed them as soon they came into the sanctuary. Immediately, the Holy Spirit began to pull me towards these two people. I did not minister to them right away, but I waited until after Joanna preached and we invited the people to come forward for prayer. I noticed this father and his son did not come to the prayer line during the invitation.

I found out later why the Holy Spirit was causing them to stand out to me. We discovered that the dad was Baptist, and he didn't believe he could be healed, but he really needed a healing in his back. He got injured protecting his son when he was a little boy. They were out playing in the snow.

He had his son on a sled, and they were sliding down a big hill. The sled got to going so fast and was heading down toward the street below. The father knew there were cars driving down the street and he could see his son was going to hit one head on. For the dad to save his son, he jumped in front of the sled taking the full blunt of the impact. His body went one way, and the sled and boy went the other way. Thank God he stopped his son from being run over by a car, but at the same time, he hurt his back really bad.

Now here they were sitting in the meeting, watching us pray for people and seeing God heal them. The son went to this church, and he was so excited when his mom and dad showed up. He kept asking his dad to go down for prayer. His father said he didn't believe in it. He even told his wife that they need to go to the church to get their son out of the cult.

I kept having this strong feeling that I need to pray for this man, so I said, "Sir, sitting right back there, could we pray for you?"

He pointed at himself and said, "Me?"

I said, "Yes sir, you."

We started praying for this man's back. I remember praying for him with my hand on his lower back. While I was praying, my hands got extremely hot. His back got so hot that I almost had to take my hands off him.

The man cried out, "What are you doing to me? What is that? What is it? What's happening?!" He thought I was putting something hot on him.

Many times, we have seen the fire of God come upon people in this way as we have prayed for them.

I said, "No sir, it's just my hand." I showed him we did not have any device in our hands. I kept praying and when I was done, I said to him, "Now see how that feels. Try to do something that you could not do before you came to this meeting."

Now remember, this man was Baptist, and he had no idea how God works when it comes to receiving divine healing. He stood up hesitantly and began to twist a little bit. Then he began to do knee squats.

Through the years we have seen many people get healed who, at the time, did not think they would be healed. It is amazing to watch as they become dumbfounded. They become speechless and almost beside themselves when they experience the touch of God.

He couldn't believe this was for real. He asked if it would last. He said, "My son had been telling me

God would heal me."

The son was crying hard and was so excited. He had always blamed himself because he was the reason his dad was in pain. Now his dad was healed, and the son got set free from blame and guilt. The joy that I saw come upon this man was incredible.

He started running all over that sanctuary and all through the church. He ran up the stairs and down the stairs, just like it was nothing. He was just laughing and having a ball. I'll never forget the look that was on his son's face as he saw his dad acting like a young child. **"It's a Miracle!"**

.

# CHAPTER NINE

# IT WAS WORTH THE DRIVE
## (Randy Herndon)

We were conducting meetings in Florida. At one gathering there was approximately 300 people in attendance. As we were praying for people in the prayer line, this young man came up to me, and said, "I don't really need anything myself, but I have a very good friend that hurt his shoulder. He cannot work because of this injury."

I said, "Where is he?"

"He's not here, but I can call him. He's 45 minutes from here."

I said, "Really? I'll tell you what you do, you

call him, and see if you can get him to drive over here and if we are done with the service, I will stay right here with you and wait for him to arrive."

He shot out of there to call his friend. I told him to holler at me when his friend arrived.

Well, of course the service kept going. We kept praying for people and it took a whole lot longer than 45 minutes.

Suddenly in the back of the room, I see him and he's waving his hand, pointing at this tall guy next to him.

I called out to him, and I said, "Well, bring him up here in the prayer line."

They came up to where I was standing, and the man introduced his friend to me. This friend told me how he got hurt when a ladder fell on him. The young man was involved in construction, and he could not work with his shoulder being so damaged.

I said, "Well, the Lord's going to heal you today. Do you believe that?"

He said, "Yes, sir. I sure do. That's why I drove over here."

He was serious, and he was not even a

Christian. He believed because his friend told him about all the **Miracle**s and healings that were happening at this church.

We prayed for him, and I said, "Now raise your arm up and down."

When this young man did that, his eyes got big. He said, "Oh, this is wonderful. I can go back to work now."

It turned out that his wife and children were banking on him to pay their bills and to feed them. God is so good even to those who have not yet made a commitment to Him. The good news is that this young man gave his heart to the Lord as a result of his healing. **"It's a Miracle!**

# LOOSE 'EM AND LET 'EM GO

We were in Richmond, Virginia speaking at a church we have gone to several times. A lady was brought to the meeting in a wheelchair-accessible van to be loaded and unloaded. I don't know what all was wrong with her, but she was bent over, and her legs were twisted. She needed a lot of help to get in and out of the van and to come to the service.

She was a member of this church, but for some reason she had not been to any of our other meetings. She finally showed up for this meeting. In this meeting there had been many healed of many different afflictions, including cancer. The word had begun to spread that **Miracle**s were happening in the church services.

After I finished preaching, I said, "We're going to pray for the sick. So, if you would like to get prayed for, please come and we will lay hands on you."

Because this was Sunday morning, and we knew that many could not stay, I also informed them that we would be holding another healing service that night, and we were also going to be sharing some miraculous testimonies of those whom God had healed and delivered.

This lady they brought in the wheelchair was bent over in a terrible way. She reminded me of the woman that Jesus prayed for in the book of Luke.

---

*"And behold, there was a woman which has a spirit of infirmity eighteen years, and was bowed together, and*

> *could in no wase lift up herself. And when Jesus saw her, he called her to him, and said unto her, 'Woman, thou are loosed from thing infirmity.' And he laid his hands on her; and immediately she was made straight, and glorified God."*
>
> *Luke 13:11-13*

---

When she talked to you, she could only look up a little. Not only was she bent over but her legs were all twisted, and she could not walk. I remember walking over to her. I did not have any information about her, but I knew it was God's will for her to be healed. I had to lean down to communicate with her because even though she was being held up by two strong men, she was bent over looking at the floor.

I said, "You know, there's a woman in the Bible that was like you. She had been bent over for 18 long years. Do you know what Jesus said to her? He said, 'Daughter of Abraham, be loosed from thine infirmity.' Jesus told Satan, 'loose her and let her go'. Now, I believe that God wants to heal you. Do you believe that?"

She said, "I don't know."

I said, "Well I do. If He did it for a woman who had been bent over for 18 long years, why wouldn't He do it for you? I believe He will heal you."

I grabbed a hold of her shoulders and I said, "In the name of Jesus!" I was pulling upwards on her shoulders as I was speaking, but at the same time, I was also pushing against that devil.

I said, "In the name of Jesus, Satan, you lose her and let her go!" At the same time I was pushing, I was thinking, 'Joanna, don't do that. You could break bones in her body.' But then I'm like, 'No Satan, you're going to let go of her.'

It's almost like I could feel this warfare going on, but I wasn't going to give up because God was going to raise her up.

I could feel the devil trying to say, "You better be careful. You're going to hurt her."

I'm like, "No, I'm not."

My husband, Randy, kind of made fun of me later. He said, "You were acting just like your dad would do in his tent meetings." He said this because sometimes my dad used to get rough and be forceful with the people who needed a **Miracle**. He would not take no for an answer because he knew God's will was to heal the people that he prayed for.

I grabbed this woman and began to command for her to be healed. I said, "You're coming up in Jesus' name!" I was holding on to her and pushing and saying, "You're coming up!"

As I did this something began to happen to her body. It had to be God because her back had been locked in place. I could see her coming up, coming up, coming up.

I said, "Keep going, keep going. God's doing it."

She kept coming up until she was looking at me in the face with tears rolling down her face and saying "I can see you. I'm not looking down at the floor anymore. I can see you."

I was about to cry with her. I hugged her and I grabbed her, and I said, "Yes, look, if God can do this with your back, then you can walk."

She looked at me kind of funny. I said, "Are you ready to walk?"

I turned to those guys who were holding on to her. I told one of them to stay on one side and I got on the other side. We grabbed a hold of her, and we were helping her. She was very wobbly and twisted in her walking. We walked with her to one side of the church and then we turned around and walked her all the way across to the other side of the church.

At first it was a little hard because her weight was pulling us down. It was kind of like lifting dead weight. But I could feel that each time we walked, she kept getting stronger. Suddenly I realized that she was no longer pulling us down with the weight of her body. She was doing the walking and we were just kind of helping her keep her balance.

We walked her a couple of times side to side in the front. We would get to one side and then we would walk all the way back to the other side. We made one more round and then I stopped with her, and I said, "You know what? If you can walk, you can run."

And she said, "Let go of me."

I thought, 'What? You don't want to run?'

She said it again, "Let go of me."

I thought maybe she was upset. Or she thought it was enough and she didn't want any more help. Then she says, "Because I want to do it all by myself."

She started moving forwards and backwards like she might fall, but she didn't. Suddenly she took off and she started running around that church. She ran and ran around the church.

The church looked like popcorn popping up and down with people jumping up and down with joy and excitement. These people were jumping up and down in their seats because they knew this woman. They had just seen an amazing **Miracle** upon one of their own church members. They saw God loose her and let her go.

The devil wants to bind you in your sickness. He wants to bind you in your sin. He wants to torment you and bind you in your mind. He will hold on to you and lock you down if you let him. But God is saying, 'Loose 'em and let 'em go!' Jesus Christ wants to loose us and set us free. What did God do for the children of Abraham, Isaac, and Jacob? He told Moses to go tell Pharaoh to *"let My people go."* **(See Exodus 8:1.)**

I believe sometimes God looks down from heaven and he says, "Devil, let my people go." God wants to loose you. He wants to set you free. You and I must come to the same place that the children of Israel finally came to. In their hearts they began to cry out to God and said, "Enough, is enough, is enough!" They said in their hearts, "I want to live. I want to be free. I want out of this bondage."

I believe we're stepping into a time and season that we're going to be loosed from all the lies of the devil. We're stepping into this day and age where God is saying, it's time for you to be loosed and let go. He hears your cries, and He sees your hunger.

There are two things that God responds to. It is the cries of His people, and the hunger of His people. He says, "I hear a cry."

Now you can let the devil keep bullying you or you can cry out to Jesus to set you free and heal you. I believe we're stepping into a season of **Miracle**s. It is not going to just be my dad's stories and our stories, but I believe you are going to have your own stories. We're not taking this anymore, because the healer, Jesus Christ is here in our midst. **"It's a Miracle!"**

# RETEST ME

**(Randy Herndon)**

We were ministering at Spirit of Life Ministries in Kingman, Indiana. Pastor Steve and Becky Crum are very good friends of ours.

There was a lady in the meeting who was in the line to be prayed for. I walked up to her, and I said, "What is wrong with you? You really look like you're sick."

She said, "I am, and I can't get well. I've been going to the doctor for some time now to get well, but nothing is working."

I said, "What are they treating you for?"

She told me the medical name. When she told me the sickness that she was dealing with (according to the doctors), something strange and amazing came out of my mouth. I immediately said, "No, that is not your problem, it's this."

I named some long medical term that I cannot even remember to this day. There's no way in the natural that I would have even known what this disease was, let alone know the medical term for it. But I just blurted it right out without even thinking.

When I told this lady this medical word for what she had, she looked at me almost in disbelief. She said to me, "Well, then what should I do?"

I said, "Well, I'll tell you what the Holy Spirit is saying to me. Go back to your doctors, and you tell them this is what you have."

I named that name again. She took a piece of paper and a pen, and she wrote what I said. It probably was misspelled, but I didn't know.

To make a long story short, she went back to the doctor and told him what I said. Of course, right away the doctor said, "Oh, no, no, no, no, no, no, no! You don't know. Who told you that?"

She said, "A man who was ministering at our church told me."

The doctor asked, "Does he have a medical license?"

She said, "No, but I believe he hears from God."

The doctor says, "What, you trust this man?"

She goes, "Yes, I do."

He said, "Okay, we'll retest you. It's may cost you because your insurance may not cover this procedure again."

She told him, "I'll pay for it."

So, they tested her again. After they had done all the tests, they told her that they would let her know when they got the results.

One day the doctor called her, and he asked her to come back into his office. When she got to the office, the doctor informed her that they were going to test her all over again.

She goes, "Oh, I can't afford another one."

He said, "No, no, no, this one's on us." So, he tested her again. Then he tested her again for a third time.

She asked, "What is going on?"

The doctor said, "Well, I don't know who that man is who told you that you had this particular affliction, but he was right on the money. That's exactly what's wrong with you." He changed her prescriptions, and she was way better within a very short time.

Now you're asking why the Lord did not just heal her instead of giving you the name of the affliction that she had? To be honest with you, I don't know. I don't have a clue. I'm not the healer. All I know is that within few weeks, she was on the road to recovery.

Now you're asking, why did I go totally against the medical profession or that doctor. It is because God gave me a supernatural word of knowledge of what was going on in her body.

Remember, the Lord numbers every hair on your head, so surely, he knows everything that is happening within us.

When we arrived at the church a few months later, she came running over to me so excited to tell me the good news of her healing. **"It's a Miracle!"**

## SHE LIVED TO TELL HER STORY

I want to share a testimony with you of a lady who was miraculously healed in my father's tent in Little Rock, Arkansas, on August 25, 1951. She lived many years after her glorious **Miracle**, into her late 80s or early 90s. Her name was Jackie Rhodes.

Jackie Rhodes and her sister, Ida, lived in a quiet town 100 miles outside of Little Rock, Arkansas. They had their own business and lived next door to their store.

Jackie's son was in the navy. They both looked forward to letters and phone calls from Jackie's son, Sonny. They were well known in the community and loved going to church.

Everything seem to be going well, but then a

fatal turn of events began to take place for Jackie Rhodes. In October 1950, she became very stiff and sore in her joints. Her joints became enlarged and grew worse and worse. She went to the most prominent doctors in Arkansas, and no one could find anything organically wrong with her, and she did not run any fever at any time.

She had x-rays, fluoroscopes, blood tests, skin test, and complete check-ups. She went to one clinic after another, and had many chiropractor adjustments, all with no results. By this time, she knew she was losing ground fast, so her family physician advised her to go to the Mayo Clinic.

In March 1951, she was diagnosed with a rare disease called Scleroderma, which involved a hardening and tightening of the skin. Her skin would literally stick to her bones. It would become so tight and get so hard that it would prevent her blood from circulating properly and so parts of her body would turn black and become hard as a stone.

After a four-day examination at the Mayo Clinic, the doctor called her sister, Ida, out into the hall and told her, "We cannot help your sister. You can take Jackie home at any time."

Twenty-five skin specialists were called in, but

they could offer nothing. They gave her light therapy as well as skin massages with cocoa butter, but it didn't help much. Her whole body began turning to stone. She could hardly open her mouth to eat or drink anything.

She had no appetite and lost a lot of weight. Her hair and eyebrows were falling out. Because her blood was not circulating properly, she could not feel the change in temperature from hot to cold. She would lay lifeless for hours at a time in a deep sleep. The skin on her chin was stuck and one side of her face was drawn out of shape. The nurse would apply therapy and massage twice daily because her skin would become so dry between treatments that it terrified her with itching. She could not stand the touch of clothing or bed-clothing.

She laid in bed for five months with just a man's vest on. Her throat begun to close as it stuck, and she knew then the disease was in the last stage of life. She turned black all over and was mentally ill. She could not think or talk clearly. She was living in a fog and could not even stand up.

She weighed 85 pounds, and she was not responding to any treatments. The doctors told the family that she only had a few days to live. Jackie's son was able to get an emergency leave form the navy to come be with her during this last stage of life.

On Sonny's way home to be with his mother, he heard about a big tent meeting in Little Rock, Arkansas. He heard about people coming out of wheelchairs, off hospital beds, blind eyes being open, the lame walking, deaf ears being opened, and so much more.

Her son talked it over with his mother and said I've heard great **Miracles** are happening there. They called their pastor and asked him what he thought about going to this tent meeting. The pastor said if it's everything you are telling me-what have you got to lose.

They had never been to a Divine healing service before, but they decided to go. This was her only hope.

Sonny, Ida, and a close friend took Jackie by car. They made a bed for her in the back seat. When they arrived, her son carried her under the tent and put her on a stretcher.

Brother Coe went up to her and said, "Do you believe that Jesus can heal you"

She said, "Yes."

Brother Coe said, "In the name of Jesus sit up."

Immediately she sat up and began to feel healing virtue flow through her whole body. She knew she was healed in that moment.

Brother Coe said to her, "Do you believe you are healed?"

She told him, "Yes."

He said, "In the name of Jesus, get up and walk."

She sat up and then stood up and started walking. She felt strength in her body and knew she was healed. Her sister tried to put her back on the stretcher after she had walked all around the tent. My dad told her sister not to put her back to bed, that Jesus just got her up.

He said to Jackie, "You will begin to eat and each day you will become stronger." He gave them instructions of things to do for the next two weeks.

They got home at 2:00 am on Sunday and was able to attend Sunday school and church that morning. Her pastor and church members were so surprised and excited to see her. They saw a **Miracle** right before their eyes. They knew it was the work of the Lord.

Jackie was raised in a Methodist church, but

she went everywhere telling people of her divine healing which she received by faith.

She could now eat anything she wanted to eat, and she felt fine. She had no pain whatsoever and the skin all over her body was loose and normal in color. She took water baths and could perspire again. She began to drive, work, type, play the piano, sew, cook, wash, iron, mop, sweep, and do many other normal activities that she used to do before her disease. She realized as she grew in faith, she grew in health. She became strong and healthy and gained 35 pounds.

She said her family doctor told her that God was the only one who could have saved her, that no medicine or human hands could have done this for her. For two years the medical doctors and hospitals would contact her as to how she got healed of this incurable disease. She would send this testimony saying, "When Brother Coe prayed for me, the disease was instantly killed."

Jackie Rhodes and her sister traveled a lot with the tent sharing her testimony. She was later hired to work in the office for my father. I would talk to her and ask her questions about her **Miracle**.

She would say, "Feel my fingers." When I felt

her fingers, they were hard as stone.

"Why are your fingers so hard like that?" I asked.

She said that God told her to let people feel her fingers to show how her body was like stone. It was a sign of her **Miracle**. What was so amazing is her fingers felt like they would not be able to move being that hard, but her fingers and every other part of her body were moving and functioning as normal. It was so amazing. She could type 90 words a minute, play the piano, sew, and stitch, and do everything anyone else could do. **"It's a Miracle!"**

## STEPPED ON HIS TWISTED FOOT

I'll never forget this one healing meeting in Corpus Christi, Texas. I told you a little earlier in this book about the Selena auditorium and several churches that had come together for healing meetings. One of the main churches that had set up that meeting have adopted us, you might say. They keep having us come back year after year, meeting after meeting. Sometimes they will have us twice a year.

Every time we've gone there, we have experienced wonderful **Miracle**s.

In one of our meetings, we encountered a lady who had Lupus who was a real estate agent. Her name is Jean Marie.

We prayed for her, and she went back to the doctors, and they tested her again. She went back to the church telling everyone that her levels went from 90 to 0 and she didn't have Lupus anymore. She was so excited, telling everyone she had been healed of Lupus. (The pastors called later and told us the report.)

These were some exciting meetings, and we were coming back to the church that had sponsored these meetings to minister. They had asked my husband and I to come and minister from Sunday through Wednesday at their church. I thought that since I preach healing and revival a lot, I would line up a theme of messages that was not about healing or revival for these meetings.

As we got close to the church where we would be ministering, I began to see these great big signs. They boldly announced, "Healing Services! Bring the sick, the lame, the diseased."

As I saw these signs, I was thinking, 'Oh, I'm

not preaching about healing.' I point to the signs, and I say to my husband, "Oh, honey, look, they are expecting healing and **Miracle** meetings."

We finally arrived in the church parking lot. As I was getting out of the car, I looked over to the left of me, and there was a woman helping a man out of a car. His foot was grossly twisted up against his leg. His one arm was drawn up close to his body, and it was twisted and mangled.

The woman who was there with him was trying to help him, but he was pushing her away. I assumed he must have been a strong, self-made man, who wanted to do it by himself. He couldn't walk because his whole foot was turned upward in an impossible angle. He literally had to walk on his ankle.

As I was watching what was going on in the parking lot, I walked up to the church door and I thought to myself, 'Oh God, these people are coming for a healing service.' While I was thinking this, somebody else pulled up to the church with a person in a wheelchair.

I said to the Lord, "Oh Lord, what are we going to speak on? Because I have all my notes on an entirely different subject. What are you going to do? This is not what I was planning, but these people who are arriving are planning on it."

I have discovered through the years that we have seen God move in healing and **Miracles** when we preach on the subject of healing.

I stepped inside of the church because the service was going to be starting soon and I needed to get alone with the Lord and pray to see what He would say to me. This church had a very steep set of stairs that you had to climb to get into the sanctuary. There was an elevator in the church that people could use but it was not working.

I was telling some of the church staff that they were going to have a real problem. I said, "There are people in wheelchairs that need to find a way to get in. Plus, there is a man who is crippled, and he is walking on his ankle. He has a twisted foot and his whole body is crippled. He is not going to be able to climb these stairs." I was trying to think about a solution for these people who would not be able to get into the main church service.

The pastors were saying they might be able to put a TV in the lobby where they could watch what was happening upstairs. During this time, the maintenance crew was trying to fix the elevator. They said there was something wrong with the hydraulics, and the fluid was low, so they were trying to get their hands on some more elevator fluid to use.

Someone finally came with some hydraulic fluid and put it in the elevator. They put a couple of people in wheelchairs, and a couple of people with crutches in the elevator and the elevator got stuck halfway up.

So, they said, "Okay, well, what are we going to do now?"

Well, four guys said, "We'll carry this man with the crippled body and twisted foot up those stairs so he can be in the service". So, they all picked this man up and carried him up.

I thought to myself, 'We are going to have to pray trauma and drama off the people in the elevator, by the time we get them into the sanctuary.'

In the meantime, they've carried this man up, and they get him all comfortable. They are still trying to get these people up and out of the elevator. A group of us all went over to the elevator and began to lay our hands on it, asking God to get the elevator to come on up.

As we were praying, you could hear the elevator beginning to slowly start back up.

Slowly it started coming up the shaft. It turned out that the elevator stopped halfway up because it still did not have enough fluid in the hydraulic system. When they put more fluid into the system, it began to climb up slowly, but surely to the main sanctuary.

Of course, the people who were on the elevator were quite upset. They were talking about how in the world they were going to get down when the service was over. Some of them were saying that they would never get back on that elevator again. There was so much trauma and drama taking place right before the service began that we had to just start praying right then and there for them.

They finally got this crippled man up into the sanctuary, but suddenly, he said that he desperately needed to get to the bathroom. Well, the bathroom was downstairs, so the same guys that had just carried him up the stairs had to pick him back up and carry him back down the stairs. After this man was finished in the bathroom, they picked him back up and carried him up the stairs again.

All kinds of things were happening. The enemy was working overtime, trying to block healings and **Miracle**s for this healing service. The people who were coming were extremely excited because they had already heard the testimonies from people who had been at our previous healing meetings. These people were coming expecting God to do **Miracle**s for them. And now here was the devil trying to fight people to stop them from getting their **Miracle** and healing.

I told these people who had been stuck in the elevator, "Now, look, you got stuck in the elevator, and you were in no condition to get up the stairs. I mean, the devil will do anything he can to keep you from getting your **Miracle**, your healing, and your deliverance."

As I was speaking to these people, God did a shift and began to change my message. I got up to preach, the Lord changed everything. It seemed like my message was directed to the man who was crippled with the twisted foot. My whole message was centered on ministering about how God stopped for the one man at the pool of Bethesda.

I can't even remember what all the message was about, but I said, "Oh Lord, this is good. Wow. This is good." And I just kept preaching.

When I finished, I said, "Sir, you with that twisted foot, come here."

I told the men who had carried him earlier, "You men help him come up here to the front for prayer."

I told this crippled man, "I believe that God is speaking a lot to you today. I believe God's going to heal you. I believe that everything's going to change." He came up front to be prayed for and I asked him, "Have you ever accepted Jesus Christ as the Lord of your life?"

He said, "No."

I asked, "Would you like to invite Jesus into your heart?"

He responded that he would like to do that. So, the first thing I did was lead him in the prayer of salvation in giving his heart to Jesus.

I said, "Anyone else here who does not know Jesus as your Savior, who has not invited Him into their heart, let's all pray together. If you mean it from your heart, it will happen. Jesus will become the Lord of your life. But if you're just saying it as a prayer to repeat, they are just words that will not impact you."

As I explained salvation and prayed with this man, tears began to stream down his face as he gave his heart to Christ with all sincerity. After that, I began to pray for his foot. I said, "I believe that God is going to do a **Miracle**. The bones in your foot are going to go snap, crackle, pop and it will be done."

We were rubbing our hands up and down his foot, across his ankle and part of his leg. You could see where he rubbed it raw by walking on that ankle. We were praying that Jesus would turn this foot around.

I reminded Jesus about the time in my dad's tent where the man's foot was turned entirely backward. As my dad was praying, that foot began to spin on his leg. Everybody saw that foot spinning. When that foot stopped spinning, it was facing frontward like any normal foot.

I said, "Lord, you did it for that man, now please do it for this man."

I had my hand running up and down his leg and on his foot, and he began to scream, "Oh, oh, oh!"

I said, "Are we hurting you?"

All that was coming out of his mouth was, "Oh! Oh!"

I said, "Oh, I'm sorry. We don't mean to hurt you."

The Lord said, "No, the devils mad. He is mad

because you're touching him and praying for a **Miracle**. Don't take your hands off."

I told the man, "I'm sorry. I don't mean to hurt you, but I have to keep doing this."

By this time, everybody that was around me was looking at me. I said to those who were staring at me, "Y'all I'm not trying to hurt him, but the devil does not like what we are doing. We are just going to keep praying for him."

So, we just kept moving our hands over his foot and he continued to shout out with pain. As we were praying, suddenly the peace of God came upon him. We then had a release to go and pray for someone else.

We went over and prayed for a lady. As we prayed for her, she came out of her wheelchair. Then we went and prayed for another one who was on crutches. This person was one of the ones on the elevator, and we prayed that the trauma and drama would come off them. At that moment, you could sense a mighty move of God amid the people. Things just began to happen rapidly. It was very busy, and people were getting healed. Backs and necks and bones were being made whole.

There was a little boy who had a rash on his

body. We were told later that this rash disappeared by the next day, but the itchiness that he was experiencing had stopped that day.

The service came to an end, but I was still dissatisfied that I did not see the man with the bent foot completely made whole. I felt the sermon was designed for this man. The minute we had pulled up into the driveway and I saw this man getting out of the car, everything changed. The atmosphere changed and my whole message changed. This man was a major part of what God was doing that day, but it seemed like he was going to be going home the way he came.

I asked this man's wife what had happened.

She said, "The doctors don't know. Suddenly his body became this way."

I said, "Okay, is it MD? Is it MS? Did he have a stroke?" They knew that it was not a stroke.

I was going through the list trying to figure out why this man had this affliction on this side of his body. The medical world did not know what it was. Even his speech was not working correctly. He could barely talk to me. His wife said that she was a nurse. She had no idea what was going on in his body either.

Something within my heart just would not let me let this man go home in the condition he was in. I said to this man again, "Do you believe God's going to heal you?"

And he said, "I guess."

I said, "I know He is going to heal you!" I kept thinking, 'Hurry up, God.'

Well, they finally left to go home. My husband and I went out to eat afterwards, but I could not enjoy my meal because I was still upset.

I kept asking God, "What about that man, Lord? I just knew You were going to do something for him because You used him to bring the inspiration for my sermon today. I know you wanted to heal that man. Why is the enemy still afflicting him?" I was upset, disappointed, and having a little pity party.

What was happening was that I was moved with compassion for this man. Jesus moved with compassion and healed the sick. It was the compassion of Christ at work inside of me for that man. Well, that night came, and we were getting ready to begin service. We had some of the people sharing their wonderful testimonies of what God had already done for them.

The worship service hadn't started yet, but we were taking a little bit of time beforehand to share what Christ had done for the people that morning. As the testimonies were taking place, guess who walked into the room? This crippled man came walking into the sanctuary all by himself. Amazingly he was completely whole. His foot was normal, and so was his arm and his hand.

I said to him, "What happened to you? Come up here and tell us what happened."

He said, "Well, I knew when you were praying, and I was in pain that the devil was trying to stop me from receiving my healing. You kept repeating that over and over to me, and it got into my heart. When I got home, I began to praise God that I was healed, even though I could not clearly state these words, it was coming from my heart. I said to myself, 'Well, if God wants to heal me, why is this foot twisted up like it is? It needs to turn down to be normal.' I said, 'God, You're going to do it. You said You were going to do it, and she said You were going to do it. And so, You are.'"

He said, "I told my wife, who is a nurse, 'Honey, I know what's wrong. If you stand on my foot, I'm going to get up. I'm going to pop it in place, and it'll be fine."

She said, "No, we can't do that. I'm a nurse, and you are not going to do that."

He told her, "No, I'm telling you, you get on my foot right now, and you stand on my foot." He was trying to tell her what to do, but he could hardly talk.

She said to him, "You don't do things like that."

He said, "Well, I'm going to do it by myself somehow, or you're going to do it for me. I'm going to put something heavy on it, and I'm going to pop it into place, but I would rather have you stand on it while I try to stand up and pop it into place." He said, "Something's blocking it, and it is going to have to loose my foot now."

His wife interjected at telling this story and told us, "I thought, as a nurse, that this was insane and crazy. To tell you the honest truth, I do not know why I cooperated with him, but I did. I finally stood up on his twisted and bent foot."

He told her, "Now hold on to something tight. Don't let me lift you off."

His wife told us that he had been a strong man before this happened. He told her, "I want you to stay on my foot no matter what you think or hear."

She said she held tightly onto the kitchen counter. When she was holding on tight, he boldly declared to the Lord, "We are doing this in your honor." Then with all of his might, he stood up. The minute he did, they heard a loud snap. It sounded like something broke. When the wife looked down, the foot was back where it belonged. At that moment, she thought he had broken bones and she thought that she needed to rush him to the hospital. She thought that he was going to pass out, but, it was the opposite.

She said to him, "Well, how are you?"

He responded to her without even a slur in his words. He said, "I told you it would work!"

She said, "Talk to me some more."

"What do you want to talk about?" he asked her.

Suddenly his arm straightened up and became normal. His hand, which had been snarled up and deformed looking, began to open.

She's like, "oh my goodness!" She said that she had just started running all over the place. She said, "I'm thinking like a nurse, I need to check his heart rate. I need to check his blood pressure. He just turned his whole foot. He could have all kinds of things wrong with him."

She said, "As a nurse, I'm thinking that. But in my heart, I knew that I did not need to test anything. God had healed my husband."

He came up those stairs that night all by himself to tell us the story. From that moment forward, they kept coming to our church services. His wife said several times he tried to commit suicide, because of his twisted body and infirmity. Not only did he get radically saved and on fire for God, but he "Hot Dog Got It!"

The next day he went to the doctor's office. He walked in under his own power, completely made whole. They had been running weeks of test or even longer and could not find out what was wrong with him. When he walked into that office, they saw him and could tell right away he was totally normal. They asked him precisely what happened to make him whole.

He said, "I went to church, and God healed me." And he began to tell them the story of how the men carried him up the stairs, carried him back down the stairs to the bathroom and carried him back up the stairs and how that we told him God was going to heal him.

He then told them how he was at home, and the idea came to him, 'I need to do something. God has healed me, but I need to do something.' He told them, "I made my wife stand on my foot, and we popped it into place. After we did that, everything else came into place."

Guess who was at church that night? The doctor! Guess who told people about the meeting on Tuesday night? The doctor! The doctor began to bring some of his patients to the meetings because he saw people that he knew were sick, being healed before his very eyes. **"It's a Miracle!**

# CHAPTER TEN
## AN AMAZING CREATIVE MIRACLE

We were in Oklahoma one time and decided to call our pastor friends. We always like to go eat and visit with them when we are close enough. We'd been there several times before, and every time we go there, we've experienced a move of God and healing **Miracle**s.

The pastor stated they were in revival and not having any speakers at this time. After a moment of silence, he said to come on anyway and minister at the church. He said, "I trust you and Randy to impart in this revival."

Sometimes there seems to be places where **Miracle**s happen more than others. This is one of those places. This pastor has always told us to contact them anytime we are coming through.

There definitely was a revival move stirring in their church. You could feel it in the atmosphere. They had people calling during worship who were being prayed for and receiving their healing by phone.

After worship, the pastor turned the meeting over to Randy and me. When I finished preaching, I told everyone that needed prayer for healing, **Miracle**s, jobs, finances, family, marriage, and more; to come to the front for prayer.

This one lady was there for prayer I had prayed for her the last time I was at this church, and she had a **Miracle** then. She had a problem and was having to use a walker. Her equilibrium was all messed up, and she would feel like she was falling or lopsided.

She had to have the walker to keep her from falling. It was so bad that she sometimes fell even with the walker. Sometimes it would throw her off balance, and she would fall. She told me that she had to use this walker because of the situation.

She said, "Would you pray for my equilibrium? Because it's not working right."

I said, "Sure." I also noticed that one side of her face was all drawn up. I said, "Well, what happened to you?"

She said, "Well, I had a tumor. They had to operate to take out this tumor. They removed this side of my face to get all that tumor out of my brain and out of my head." She informed me that this is why her face was all drawn up to her eye.

As I looked at her face, it was evident that she must have had reconstructed surgery after that major surgery.

I prayed for her equilibrium. After praying I said, "Let's see how your walking is now." We went walking first with the walker and then without the walker. She was apprehensive without the walker at first, but when she realized she was not off balance and she could walk all over, she was so excited!

She said, "Look at this, this is great and I'm not losing my balance." She tested turning around because she said that always threw her off balance, but it didn't. God did a **Miracle** for her.

So, now we're back here again, and here she is, and she's walker free and not losing her balance. She is still healed of the equilibrium problems.

This time, she walked up to me, and she said, "I need you to pray." There was something she asked me to pray for. And I really cannot remember what it was. I reached up to ask her something in her left ear. She said, "Oh, I don't know what you said to me. I can't hear out of that ear. You'll have to talk to me in the other ear."

I said, "Oh really?" I forgot what she had originally asked prayer for because now I wanted her to hear out of this ear.

I said, "That's okay I'm going to pray for you to hear."

A determination hit my heart for God to give her healing in that ear. I reached up and put my hand on her ear and began praying for her ear to open to hear in Jesus' name! Then I leaned forward to her and said, "You are going to hear out of that ear!" Then I whispered in her ear, "Jesus loves you."

She said, "Honey I don't know what you are saying because I told you to speak to me in my other ear. I cannot hear out of that ear because I don't have an ear."

I said, "Yes you do have an ear and you are
going to hear, because I'm going to pray
again. So, I reached up, and I started praying
for that ear in the name of Jesus. "Right now,
we ask You, Lord Jesus, to heal this ear.
Open up this ear that she can hear out of it."

As I was praying over this ear she repeated to
me, "I don't know what you're saying. I know
that I can feel something of your breath on
that side of my face, but I don't know what
you're saying. I told you; I cannot understand
you when you talk to me in that ear." She
made this strange statement once again, "I
don't have an ear." As she was telling me that
she does not have an ear, I basically ignored
her.

I reached my hand back up, and I prayed
again. I said, "In the name of Jesus, Lord; I'm
asking you to open this ear that she may hear.
Lord, I know that the devil is blocking her
hearing, but Lord, open this ear."

I quoted scriptures and spoke the name of
Jesus as I was praying over this woman's ear.
When I got done praying, I put my mouth next
to her ear and whispered, "Praise the Lord!"

She was beginning to get flustered with me.
She said, "I told you I can't hear! I'm sorry, but

279

I told you, I don't have an ear to hear you. If you talk to me in the other ear, I can hear you."

I said, "I want you to hear out of this ear. So, I'm going to pray for you again."

She said, "I don't have an ear!"

I said, "Yes you do, and I'm going to pray again."

You see, I was looking at her ear. I reached up, and I prayed for that ear again. God had put a determination in my heart to get this ear healed. I am speaking healing and demanding this ear to be opened in the name of Jesus. I reached up again and whispered "Jesus" in her ear, thinking to myself, 'I may have to pray again.'

She exclaims quickly, "You just said Jesus in my ear! I heard it and I don't have an ear!" Her whole countenance and demeanor changed. It's like she went into complete shock.

I was so excited I reached up and whispered, "Jesus loves you."

She hollers, "you said Jesus loves you and I can hear you. I don't have an ear and I can hear!"

So now I'm running all over the church because God gave this woman hearing in her ear that she could not hear out of. I was so thrilled and excited that God answered our prayer.

She grabbed the pastor and pulled him down off the steps of the platform and says, "Pastor, pastor, I couldn't hear out of that ear, because I don't have an ear, but now I hear."

He looked at her face and sees the ear. He said to her, "Yes, you have an ear!"

She said in total shock and excitement, "I can hear! I can hear, and I don't have an ear!"

The pastor went over to this woman's husband who was on the stage. He was the drummer on the worship team. The pastor said to him, "Get down here. Your wife says she can hear, but she keeps saying she doesn't have an ear, but she has an ear."

So, the husband comes down and approaches his wife. He leaned over and said something in that her ear where she said she did not have an ear. She looked at her husband and repeated what he had just told her. When she repeated what he said to her, he went down under the power of God. I mean, he is out under the glory of God, laying on the floor of the sanctuary. What was happening did not make sense to any of us who were there that day. We had no idea that God had done a creative **Miracle**.

I saw the pastor standing there, like, 'what is going on?'

And I'm like, 'what happened? What? Her husband is laid out on the floor.'

The husband began to talk to me as he was laying on the floor. He repeated what she said, "She does not have an ear."

I said, "Yes, she does. I can see her ear."

He said, "No, she doesn't. What you don't understand was that the tumor that she had filled that whole side of her face. When they removed that tumor, they had to remove her ear works. The doctors removed her eardrum and ear canal. All you see is an ear, but she has no ear works."

Oh, it's a good thing that I did not know this before I began to pray for her. I might have stopped praying for that ear to be opened if I had known that they removed everything. I kept telling her, "Don't tell me that you have no ear." God did an amazing creative **Miracle** that day.

Wherever she goes, she tells the people about what God did for her on that day. She went back to the doctors and told them that she could now hear out of that ear. They would not believe her. She would tell them, "I can prove it to you." She would cover her good ear and have them talk to the ear where there was no ear.

She kept telling the doctors, but they would not believe her. She would tell them to just say something low. "I'll plug this good ear, and I'll tell you what you said." The doctors followed her instructions, but they were so full of unbelief they kept on denying that it could not be true.

Finally, one of the doctors said, "I don't understand it. We took your eardrum. Your ear works. Your ear canal out. There are no ear works."

She said, "well, I heard you, I heard you."

They said, "Well, we're going to check this out." They examined that ear from top to bottom and discovered the inner workings of that ear were completely normal. **"It's a Miracle!"**

## DYING FROM HEPATITIS BUT HEALED

We were at one of the conferences that is held every year in West Lafayette Indiana. As I was walking in the door to the church, this whole family ran up to me, almost knocking me down. They were hugging me and thanking me. The little kids were trying to climb up on me and gave me hugs and kisses. They kept saying, "Thank you, thank you, thank you!"

I'm like, "Okay, you're welcome. What did I do?"

I didn't even know them. I was trying to figure out how I knew them. I finally had to ask them what I did because I'm being bombarded by little children grabbing my leg. Some of them were trying to get closer. They kept asking me where I was going. They wanted to follow me to the bathroom.

I finally said, "What happened?"

They said, "You helped our grandma to live.

Our grandma is still here."

That is when their grandma walked up to me and said, "You don't remember me, do you? You prayed for me."

I said, "Can you tell me what happened?"

She said, "I was in about in the middle of the front line where people were being prayed for. When you finally got to where I was standing, you stopped and prayed. Up to that moment you had been hugging people and loving on them. When you came to me you touched my head and said, 'Be healed in the name of Jesus.' There was like electricity that shot through my body.

It felt like you hit me very hard, but it wasn't you I found out later, it was the power of God. When I hit the floor, my whole body began to shake violently. I fell to the floor, and I kept thinking, 'I can't stop shaking.' I was thinking, 'What did she do to me? What's wrong with me? Am I having a seizure? What is this and what's happening?' But finally, I was able to get up and I felt wonderful."

She told me she was in stage four hepatitis C. The doctors told her she needed to get her house in order. They said she wouldn't live long. The people who had brought her to church helped carry her into the building. They were holding onto her before I walked up to her. When I prayed for her, the power of God hit her, and she went down.

She said, "Before you prayed for me, I was so sick that I probably would not have made it much longer. When I got up, I felt wonderful. All the symptoms, pain and suffering were gone. I went back to the doctors to be examined and they said I do not hepatitis C anymore. It is all gone. And I'm still alive. This is why my children, and my grandchildren are so thankful for you. I would've been dead if you would not have prayed for me."

I told her, "No, it was not me that healed you, it was Dr. Jesus."

Jesus still heals hepatitis C, HIV, sexually transmitted diseases, and whatever else the enemy may throw at us. When the medical world says there is no hope, Dr. Jesus says yes. Dr. Jesus is the same yesterday, today, and forever. He gave His life so that you could be saved, healed, and delivered. **He is the Lord that healeth thee. "It's a Miracle!"**

# NO MORE BACK SURGERIES

This is an amazing **Miracle** that happened in Indiana. We were ministering on the prayer line to many of those who had come for prayer.

As my husband and I were ministering to those who had come up, we noticed a man and a woman standing on prayer line. You could tell he had helped her to get to the prayer line, but he was surrounding her with his arms to keep her inside this circle he had made for her.

The Spirit of God drew us to her. At that moment we had no idea what it was that she was facing. Later we found out that she had been in the hospital. She insisted that her husband take her to the church service that night. He tried to convince her otherwise because of her serious condition, but she insisted.

I walked up and I said, "Sir, what's wrong with your wife? Can we pray for her?"

He said, "Yes, but don't touch her."

"Okay. I won't." You could tell that he was

upset or very worried about her. I kept on gently speaking to him before we could finally break through that barrier of his protectiveness over her.

He told us, "I just got her from the hospital, from her eighth back surgery. Yes, that is correct, the eighth back operation. She has in her spine a lot of metal."

The husband had his arms still surrounding her with the circle protection. He was worried she might fall out and didn't want her to even be there. We kept telling him that we would like to pray for her. But he was extremely reluctant with us putting our hands upon her. It seemed like a very long time before we were able to talk him into letting us pray for her.

Well, we were finally able to pray for her. And one thing led to another. We knew that we could not be very forceful with this situation. It was what you'd call a generic sort of prayer.

We asked her if we could put our hands on her neck to pray. As we were praying for her neck, it started getting really hot. Randy said, "You know that heat is Jesus touching you and healing you?"

Told her to try to slowly move her head to see

how it was feeling. She started moving her head. She started moving her shoulders. Then she started moving her head back and forth, slow at first, and then faster and faster. She said, "Oh that feels good."

Randy told her, "If He's doing your neck, He's probably doing your back too."

She started twisting her whole body. When she began to do this her husband freaked out. He put his arms back around her. He was afraid that she was going to fall under the power of God. She kept moving her body every which way. We kept praying and speaking the name of Jesus over her. She began to radically twist and turn her whole body. Her husband was about to pass out because of what she was doing. He knew how bad her back was, and what the doctors had told them.

The fire of God hit this lady's body. We could literally feel the heat burning in her body as my hand was running up and down her back and over her shoulder. I asked her if she was feeling this heat. She acknowledged that she could feel the heat through her whole body.

Randy said, "I can visibly see something is happening in your neck, and that it is straightening out. God is healing your back and putting it back into its proper place."

I said, "Now gently turn your head to the side." And she did it like there was nothing wrong.

Then I said, "Now turn it the other way." She did what I told her to do and turned her head the other way. Her husband was absolutely blown away.

I said, "Now, before we prayed for you, you could not move your head or your neck, right?"

She said, "No"

I said, "Well, if God's done that for your neck, then surely, He's done something for your back. Why don't you go ahead and check out your back to see what God's done."

When I said that to her, she started twisting, jumping up and down and dancing. Her husband was in shock and said to her, "What are you doing?" Remember she had just gotten out of surgery.

From the time she was 16 years old up to this moment she had been in constant suffering. This had been her eighth major surgery on her back. It was obvious to everyone that God had done a supernatural and divine **Miracle** for her that night.

The next time we saw her was the next morning. Guess who was up in the front of the church jumping and dancing and carrying on during praise and worship? This lady! The husband was no longer behind her trying to protect her, but he was beside her worshiping God. This precious sister was just going at it, dancing, twisting, and twirling. I'm talking about the chubby checkers kind of twisting.

We heard later that she went back to the hospital for a routine checkup of her back. When the x-rays came back, they were absolutely flabbergasted. Not only was her back completely healed but all the metal they had to install in order to brace her backbone was gone. That's the way our God works. **"It's a Miracle!"**

# TOO GOOD TO NOT BELIEVE

I want to share some words from a song I heard recently. It really covers how I feel about the **Miracle**s and healing moves of God. The song is called *Too Good To Not Believe,* written by Brandon Lake and Cody Carnes. You need to get it and listen to it. Here are some of the lyrics I wanted to highlight as to why this is so powerful.

---

*I've lived stories that have proved your faithfulness*
*And I've seen Miracles my mind can't comprehend*
*And there is beauty in what I can't understand*
*Jesus, it's You, Jesus, it's You*

*I believe*
*You're the wonder-working God*
*You're the wonder-working God*
*All the Miracles I've seen*
*You're too good to not believe*
*You're the wonder-working God*
*And You heal because You love*
*Oh, the Miracles we'll see*
*You're too good not to believe*

*I can't resurrect a man with my own hands*
*But just the mention of Your name can raise the dead*
*So all the glory to the only One who can*
*Jesus, it's You, Jesus, it's You*

And I've seen cancer disappear
I've seen metal plates dissolve
Don't you tell me He can't do it
Don't you tell me He can't do it

'Cause I've seen real life resurrection
I've seen mental health restored
Don't you tell me He can't do it
Don't you tell me He can't do it

'Cause I've seen families reunited
I've seen prodigals return
Don't you tell me He can't do it
Don't you tell me He can't do it

'Cause I've seen troubled souls delivered
I've seen addicts finally free
Don't you tell me He can't do it
Don't you tell me He can't do it

We'll see cities in revival
And salvation flood the streets
Don't you tell me He can't do it
Don't you tell me He can't do it

We'll see glory fill the nations
Like the world has never seen
Don't you tell me He can't do it
Cause I know that He can

I believe

# TESTIMONIES NEVER GET OLD

Another time when we were with Pastor Steve and Becky Crum in Kingman, Indiana, Randy was up sharing a testimony of a woman who had breast cancer and what God had showed him. I was standing beside him, because when he finished sharing, I was going to preach.

Randy was telling a testimony I already knew and had heard several times. I was kind of ho-hum acting, and really just thinking about what I need to do and say whenever he finished. I was not really paying much attention to what Randy was saying but then I heard the Lord say, "Oh, so my stories get old to you?"

I replied to the Lord, "Do what?"

He said again, "So my stories get old to you? Do you get tired of hearing about the parting of the Red Sea?"

I said, "No!"

"The woman with issue of blood made whole?"

"No sir."

"The blind man on the road to Jericho who received his sight?"

"No!"

"The man at the pool of Bethesda who immediately took up his bed and walked?"

"No sir! No Lord, I do not get tired of hearing Your stories." By then I was weeping and crying. My heart and spirit were broken, and all the people were looking at me.

The Lord said to me, "Well, that's My story Randy is telling, and you are acting like it gets old because you have heard it so many times."

I was just standing there weeping and crying and asking God to forgive me for taking this so lightly. This was not Randy's story; this was God's story.

The Lord began to take me all through the Bible of the stories, with the crucifixion, the resurrection, and the ascension.

I said, "No, God." By then, I was bent over and weeping.

During this whole time, Randy was still trying to tell the story. He was looking at me because he could tell something was happening.

I was saying to God, "Oh no, no, I don't get tired of your stories, God. I'm sorry!"

He said, "I want you to know that story your husband is telling; that is My story. My stories do not get old. And you tell my people that the stories of their life, their testimonies, and their **Miracle**s do not get old. They need to tell their stories and not think they are getting old."

The devil wants you to shut up about the things God has done for you. The devil will tell you that you have said it enough, people have heard it enough and to quit telling it. I'm here to tell you that's a lie from the pits of hell. You are overcomers by your testimony and by the blood of the Lamb. You keep telling your story, because it is not your story, it's God's story.

Take time to tell of the **Miracle**s that God has done for you; how He forgave you, saved you and healed you; how He answered your prayers and supplied your needs. Every time you tell your testimony, you are telling God's story about what He has done for you. It is God's Word at work in your heart and His word will never pass away. **"It's a Miracle!**

# ENDNOTES

These are not fictitious stories, but true God stories. There are so many more testimonies and stories of the **Miracle**s and healings we have been a part of throughout our travels. The testimonies will not stop being told or happening because we continue to keep praying and believing. The greatest **Miracle** story in my life is the day Jesus saved my soul, He cleansed me, and He made me whole. He is Lord of my life! **"It's a Miracle!"**

# TO BE CONTINUED

---

# Healing Scriptures

---

*"Many are the afflictions of the righteous: but the Lord delivereth him out of them all."*

*Psalm 34:19*

---

*"O Lord my God, I cried unto thee, and thou hast healed me."*

*Psalm 30:2*

---

*"As for me, I will call upon God; and the Lord shall save me. Evening, and Morning, and at noon, will I pray, and cry aloud: and He shall hear my voice." Psalm 55:16-17*

---

*"Cast thy burden upon the Lord, and He shall sustain thee: He shall never suffer the righteous to be moved." Psalm 55:22*

---

*"Look upon mine affliction and my pain; and forgive all my sins." Psalm 25:18*

---

*"Bless the Lord, O my soul, and forget not all His benefits: who forgiveth all thine iniquities; who healeth all thy diseases; who redeemeth thy life from destruction; who crowneth thee with lovingkindness and tender mercies; who satisfieth thy mouth with good things; so that thy youth is*

*renewed like the eagle's." Psalm 103:2-5*

---

*"He sent his word, and healed them, and delivered them from their destructions." Psalm 107:20*

---

*"I shall not die, but live, and declare the works of the Lord."*

*Psalm 118:17*

---

*"Surely, he hath borne our griefs, and carried our sorrows: yet we did esteem him stricken, smitten of God, and afflicted. But He was wounded for our transgressions, He was bruised for our iniquities: the chastisement of our peace was upon him; and with His stripes we are healed." Isaiah 53:4-5*

---

*"Who his own self bare our sins in his own body on the tree, that we, being dead to sins, should live unto righteousness: by whose stripes ye were healed." 1 Peter 2:24*

---

*"Is any sick among you? Let him call for the elders of the church; and let them pray over him, anointing him with oil in the name of the Lord: And the prayer of faith shall save the sick, and the Lord shall raise him up; and if he have committed sins, they shall be forgiven him." James 5:14-15*

---

*"That it might be fulfilled which was spoken by Esaias the prophet, saying, Himself took our infirmities, and bare our sicknesses." Matthew 8:17*

*"Jesus answered and said unto them, 'Verily I say unto you, if ye have faith, and doubt not, ye shall not only do this which is done to the fig tree, but also if ye shall say unto this mountain, Be thou removed, and be thou cast into the sea; it shall be done. And all things, whatsoever ye shall ask in prayer, believing, ye shall receive.'" Matthew 21:21-22*

# ABOUT THE AUTHORS

Joanna Coe-Herndon is the daughter of legendary Healing Evangelist Jack Coe Senior. She and her husband Randy bring a life changing message of salvation, hope, healing, and restoration through faith in the Name of our Lord Jesus Christ.

The Lord has imparted to Joanna spiritual gifts identical to that of her father and given her a relevant message for this end-time generation.

Joanna and Randy believe God has called them to awaken the church to its need for true revival. Their messages are designed to inspire Godly repentance and ignite a passion to reach the lost with the love of Jesus Christ.

In all revival service lives are radically Transformed. The sick are healed, souls are saved and we encounter the presence of the Living God.

Made in the USA
Columbia, SC
26 September 2022